The Roots of Danger

MASTERS SERIES IN CRIMINOLOGY

Series Editor
Henry N. Pontell.
School of Social Ecology, University of California, Irvine

White-Collar and Corporate Crime
by Gilbert Geis

Electronic Crime
by Peter Grabosky

Chasing After Street Gangs: A Forty-Year Journey
by Malcolm W. Klein

*Juvenile Delinquency and Delinquents: The Nexus
of social Change*
by James F. Short, Jr. and Lorine A. Hughes

FORTHCOMING

*Feminist Criminology: Crime, Patriarchy,
and the Control of Women*
by Meda Chesney-Lind

The Great Punishment Experiment
by Todd R. Clear

Social support and Crime in America: A New Criminology
by Francis T. Cullen

*Social Roots of Crime: why some societies
Are More Violent Than Others*
by Elliott Currie

Developmental and Life Course Theories of Offending
by David P. Farrington

Crimes of Memory
by Elizabeth Loftus

Identity Fraud
by Henry N. Pontell

MASTERS SERIES
IN CRIMINOLOGY

The Roots of Danger: Violent Crime in Global Perspective

Elliott Currie
University of California,
Irvine

Prentice Hall
Upper Saddle River, New Jersey
Columbus, Ohio

Library of Congress Cataloging-in-Publication Data

Currie, Elliott.
  The roots of danger : violent crime in global perspective / Elliott Currie.
    p. cm.
  ISBN-13: 978-0-13-227751-8
  ISBN-10: 0-13-227751-4
  1. Violent crimes.   I. Title.
HV6493.C87 2009
364.15—dc22

2008036029

Vice President and Executive Publisher:
  Vernon Anthony
Senior Acquisitions Editor: Tim Peyton
Editorial Assistant: Alicia Kelly
Media Project Manager: Karen Bretz
Director of Marketing: David Gesell
Marketing Manager: Adam Kloza

Marketing Coordinator: Alicia Dysert
Production Manager: Wanda Rockwell
Creative Director: Jayne Conte
Cover Design: Brian Kane
Full-Service Project Management/
  Composition: Aptara, Inc
Printer/Binder: Bind-Rite/Command Web

Credits and acknowledgments borrowed from other sources and reproduced, with permission, in this textbook appear on appropriate page within text.

Pearson Education Ltd., London
Pearson Education Singapore, Pte. Ltd.
Pearson Education Canada, Ltd.
Pearson Education—Japan
Pearson Education Australia PTY, Limited

Pearson Education North Asia Ltd., Hong Kong
Pearson Educación de Mexico, S.A. de C.V.
Pearson Education Malaysia, Pte. Ltd.

Prentice Hall
is an imprint of

www.pearsonhighered.com

10 9 8 7 6 5 4 3 2 1
ISBN-13: 978-0-13-227751-8
ISBN-10:   0-13-227751-4

CONTENTS

Elliott Currie is Professor of Criminology, Law, and Society at the University of California, Irvine. He is the author of many works on crime, juvenile delinquency, drug abuse, and social policy, including *Confronting Crime* (1985); *Dope and Trouble: Portraits of Delinquent Youth* (1991); *Reckoning: Drugs, the Cities, and the American Future* (1993); *Crime and Punishment in America* (1998), which was a finalist for the 1999 Pulitzer Prize in General Nonfiction; and *The Road to Whatever: Middle Class Culture and the Crisis of Adolescence* (2005), a study of troubled middle-class youth in America. He is a coauthor of *Whitewashing Race: The Myth of a Colorblind America* (2003), a finalist for the C. Wright Mills Award of the Society for the Study of Social Problems in 2004 and winner of the 2004 Book Award from the Benjamin L. Hooks Institute for Social Change.

ACKNOWLEDGMENTS

Thanks, first of all, to Henry Pontell for conceiving this series and inviting me on board—and for thoughtful comments on the manuscript. Special thanks also to Marjon Michelle Raji for enthusiastic and helpful research assistance.

Writing this book reminded me, not for the first time, of the great debt I owe to the teachers whose encouragement and example inspired me to want to study social issues in the first place, and has kept me going ever since: Robert Blauner, David Matza, Sheldon Messinger, Jerome Skolnick, and—at the very beginning—Helena Znaniecki Lopata.

I'd like to dedicate this book to the memory of Ian Taylor—a good friend, a treasured colleague, and a committed and tough-minded advocate for a better world. Ian's work continues to inform and clarify my own. He is sorely missed.

INTRODUCTION | VIOLENCE AS A SOCIAL ISSUE

In the summer of 2007, four young students were lined up against a schoolyard wall in Newark, New Jersey. Three were killed execution style—forced to kneel on the ground, then fatally shot in the back of the head. A fourth was seriously wounded in the attack. The crime gained national attention because it seemed especially cold-blooded, and because the slain young people seemed to have such promise. But killings, unfortunately, were far from unusual in Newark. As one resident told the *New York Times*, "Murder is the norm" in that city. Fifty-seven other people had already been killed in Newark since the beginning of the year. As the newspaper report put it, "Amid the anger, tears and heartache over the recent execution-style killings of three college-bound young people in Newark, there is also a sense of resignation that the slayings are an all too familiar part of everyday life."

Newark is a tough city, but it is hardly alone in America as a place where slayings are "all-too-familiar." The same could be said of Philadelphia, Los Angeles, St. Louis, Washington, Chicago, Baltimore, Oakland, Detroit—and many others. There were 20 homicides in a single zip code in Los Angeles in just the first seven months of 2007. As the Los Angeles *Times* reported,

> People living close to frequent violent death find refuge in denial. On the same streets where sidewalks are stained by the

melted wax from homicide shrines and young men loiter in wheelchairs, people talk about being "caught slippin'" (letting one's guard down) or about friends having "passed" (not having been killed) . . .

In parts of South Los Angeles . . . there are people who have lost not one, but two or more family members. Michael Presley, 19, killed in the Los Angeles police department's Southwest Division, was buried in the same grave as his father, also a murder victim.

Theodore Giddens, 44, killed in LAPD's Newton Division on July 13, was the third member of his immediate family to be murdered. Dovon Harris was the second of his father's sons to die from homicide. Both Julio Ramirez, 21, killed in a double homicide in Paramount on July 29, and Noel Velazco, 26, killed in Southwest Division on August 9, were preceded in death by brothers who were also murdered.

"After this pain, we could lose nothing more," said Velazco's mother, speaking after her second son, twin to the first, was shot and killed only yards from where his brother had fallen six years before. (Leovy, 2007)

More Americans die of homicide every three months than the total who died in the September 11 attacks on the World Trade Center in New York or—as of this writing—in the several years of the war in Iraq. And murder is only the tip of the iceberg of violence in these cities: For every young man who dies by violence in the United States, another 75 end up in a hospital emergency room for treatment of a violence-related injury.

In much of urban America, we have become accustomed to living with violence; we tend to take it for granted, unless it takes spectacular or especially tragic forms like the senseless deaths of the students in Newark. Most violent crimes—even murders—don't even make the news. Violence is simply part of the landscape, the background of everyday life. And we adjust our own lives accordingly. We avoid certain neighborhoods altogether, if we can (and if we don't happen to live in them). We don't go out at night in some parts of our cities, at least not by ourselves. We fortify our homes and cars with bars, manned gates, and alarms. We factor in the relative risks of violence in many of our basic decisions in life—where we will live or where we will send our children to school.

It is natural to assume that the same conditions hold true everywhere else. But it is wrong. In many countries around the world, murders are far from being a familiar part of everyday life. In fact, in most other affluent industrial societies, the deliberate killing of one person by another is an extremely rare event. Most people, most of the time, go about their daily lives without much fear of violence. Their neighborhoods are not torn by drive-by shootings or by the routine sound of police helicopters in the night. There are no candles at shrines for homicide victims.

At the same time, there are other societies where violence is even more pervasive than it is in the United States. In some countries of Latin America and the Caribbean, crime and violence "constitute a human tragedy of rapidly growing proportions," as a recent study put it: one that brings "enormous social costs." According to one survey, nearly one third of girls in Jamaica are "afraid to go to school because of the threat of crime and violence" (Ayers, 1998, 1, 7). In Russia, it's estimated that more than 1 million people died from violent crime between 1987 and 2003 alone (Galinsky, 2006).

In Germany, however, according to one recent report, "violent crimes that harm the physical integrity of the individual are relatively rare," and residents' satisfaction with public safety "has never been higher" (Oberwittler and Hofer, 2005, 469, 476). In a number of other

European countries—Sweden, Denmark, Austria, Finland, and the Netherlands among them—citizens report little sense of being unsafe when "walking alone in the areas where they live at night."

No modern society is altogether without violent crime. But the variation in the risks of violence across different societies is enormous. It is often obscured, as we'll see later, by the way we measure crime. And it is sometimes downplayed for political or ideological reasons. But it is a defining feature of violent crime in our time. And it is not just an abstract or a theoretical issue—although it does tell us a great deal about what causes crime and violence and what does not. It has a profound impact on people around the world—shaping the quality of their lives and even their life expectancy.

Today, there are many places in the world where the threat of being killed, seriously injured, or sexually assaulted by another human being is minuscule; where for the most part men and women, young and old, can walk the streets at any time, day or night, with little fear. There are other places where death or serious injury from violence decimates a significant part of the population—especially the young—and is, in fact, a major cause of the loss of life. The burden of violent crime, in short, is not shared equally around the globe. It is heavily concentrated in some societies, and some places and people within those societies. And it is usually only one among many other social ills that afflict the people who live in those places.

This has important implications for how we deal with violent crime. The fact that violence varies so greatly tells us that is not inevitable—not a normal or necessary part of modern life—or an inherent aspect of human nature, as some people have argued. It tells us that there are reasons why some places are more dangerous than others. And if we can understand those reasons, then we have the most important tools to help us reduce violence and the suffering it brings. Having the tools, of course, is not the same as actually using them—doing something about the problem. That requires not only understanding, but also political will and a sense of social purpose. But understanding is a necessary first step.

That is what this short volume aims to accomplish. I don't claim to be exhaustive here. The roots of violent crime are complex, and every society's experience of it is unique, profoundly shaped by its own historical circumstances and cultural and social traditions. And there is a vast amount of research on the causes of violence—more than I can possibly cover in these pages. What I try to do here is more modest: outline some of the dimensions of violence across the world today, and then examine some common explanations for the variations in violence across different societies—both those that seem justified on the basis of the evidence and those that do not.

I should say at the start that our understanding of the problem of violence, like that of other social problems, is a work in progress. There is much we still need to learn. But we know enough to make a difference when it comes to reducing the level of violence suffered by people around the world. So even in the absence of certainty about some questions, I am prepared to make some fairly strong assertions in this book, because the situation is truly urgent. In some places—including parts of my own country—violence constitutes a genuine social and moral emergency. Violent crime takes roughly half a million lives, at a conservative estimate, around the world every year, and it disables and scars far more—both physically and emotionally (Krug, Dahlberg, Mercy, Zwi, and Lozano, 2002). And, as I said, it does so unequally—unfairly—striking some people in some places far more than others. In some parts of the world, violence is sufficiently pervasive that it interferes with social and economic development—and therefore creates a vicious downward spiral in which poor social conditions create high levels of violence, which in turn exacerbate those adverse social conditions and inhibit the possibility of rising above them.

Violent crime is not only a social problem and an economic problem, not only a public health problem or a problem for criminal justice agencies, but also a moral problem—especially because it is a largely *preventable* problem. Our failure to do more to prevent violence on the basis of what we already know about its causes condemns great numbers of people around the world to needless suffering and, all too often, premature death. In that sense, we must think of our failure to act as a violation of fundamental human rights.

What keeps us from acting more systematically on the knowledge we have? Partly, I believe, it's because we suffer from a kind of myopia about violent crime. Because we rarely look past our own country's experience, we have nothing to compare it to, so we don't see that it is not a natural or inevitable phenomenon. That myopia is exacerbated by some of our common preconceptions about crime. We often think of the people who commit crimes as just "bad people," or, as Newark's mayor put it in response to the triple shootings there, that crime is a product of "pure evil." We don't take the next step and ask where those "bad people" come from—or why there are so many of them in some places and so few in others. Or, we say it's because we're not "tough" enough on criminals—and if we just "cracked down" on them, the problem would go away. But, as we'll see later, most of the societies that suffer from high levels of violence, including the United States, are also among those with the harshest policies toward criminals. Recently, it has become fashionable (not for the first time in our history) to explain crime in terms of genetic or biological factors that distinguish criminals from other people, and to hope that science will somehow come up with ways to predict who they are and isolate them from the rest of us. But, again, not much is said about why it is that there seem to be so many of those peculiar people in some places—and not others.

Such "explanations" fail because they can't comprehend the reality of the wide variations in violence around the world. The explanations that *do* fit that reality are far less simple—which may be one reason why they don't catch the attention of the media and the public in the way that less satisfactory explanations often do. And they also point to factors that are deeply entwined with the most fundamental social, economic, and cultural patterns in a society. Changing those patterns is rarely easy, because they involve not just the heavy weight of tradition, but also entrenched and often powerful interests. The kind of endemic violence that afflicts the United States and some other countries, as we'll see later, is bred by a complex mix of social inequalities and depriv-ations that have profound effects on most aspects of peoples' lives, not just crime. Those conditions have sometimes been present for generations, and would be hard to change even with the best will in the world. But too often the best will is lacking, because while those condi-tions are obviously bad for many people, they may also benefit others—at least in the short run.

Ultimately, though, the discovery that violence has social origins that are both understandable and preventable is a hopeful one. It shows us that we are not simply stuck with the level of violence we now face. But to move beyond it, we need to separate reality from misconception: and that is a large part of what I hope to do in this book.

Let me be clear about what I mean by *violence*. I use the terms *violence* and *violent crime* interchangeably; When I talk about violence, I mean violent crime, rather than collective forms of violence, such as civil wars or revolutions. And I focus on the kinds of violent crime that take place in the streets and in the homes—not on violence committed by, say, governments or corporations—which can be terribly destructive in its own right, as well as criminal. I also focus on *serious* violent crime committed by individuals against others—not on everyday fights in the schoolyard or shoving matches in the local bar, but on the kinds of violence that can cause great physical and emotional harm: murder, rape, serious assault, and robbery.

I begin by describing the dimensions of that kind of violence, paying special attention to unraveling some of the complexities of measuring it—complexities that can mask the depth of the disparities in violence around the world. I then look at some popular—but misleading—explanations for the wide disparities in violence we see across different societies. From there, I look in more detail at several explanations that fit the evidence. None of them can do the job of explaining the unequal pattern of violence by itself, but taken together, they provide a framework that gives us a good start. I conclude by summing up what I think we've learned about the roots of violence, and take a moment to consider the implications of some of our current social and economic policies in the light of that understanding. For there is reason, unfortunately, to worry that in many countries we are moving in precisely the wrong directions if our goal is to reduce the toll of violence. We are in danger of ignoring the lessons that we've painstakingly learned through research and experience, and of dismantling some of the institutions that have helped to make some societies relatively free of violence up to now. If this book can help us avoid that, it will have served its purpose.

I | DIMENSIONS

A. MEASURING VIOLENT CRIME

I said earlier that the enormous variation in violence around the world is one of its key characteristics. But how do we know that? How do we find out how much violent crime exists in a society and how it compares with other places?

As it turns out, the answer is very complicated. Much—in fact, most—violent crime flies under the radar of authorities, in some societies more than others. As a result, almost all of our usual measures of violence understate it considerably, some measures more than others. This makes assessing violence difficult even within a single society, and more so when we try to compare different societies with each other. Some of these problems of measurement are well known and glaring; others are more subtle and less often acknowledged. Taken together, they mean that statistics on violent crime are very tricky, and often misused—sometimes in very misleading ways.

I should point out at the start that my own "take" on the problems of crime statistics may be more skeptical than that of some other people who study them. But most scholars agree that, for most kinds of violent crime, the true picture, particularly in some countries, is very difficult to uncover.

There are basically four different sources of data used by researchers to study violence around the world, and they are of very different quality and reliability. The four are crimes reported to police agencies; interview surveys of the victims of crime; "self-report" surveys that ask people to reveal how often they themselves have broken the law; and health statistics, notably "mortality" statistics, or data on the causes of death.

Let's take the police reports first. These are the statistics that are most frequently reported in the media, but they're widely regarded as among the least reliable—especially for some kinds of crimes. The basic problem with relying on data reported to police is one that's universally acknowledged: Crimes aren't counted in the statistics unless someone reports them (or the police themselves do). For a few crimes, like murder and (in some countries) car theft, that's not a big problem, because these crimes are usually reported, at least in the advanced industrial societies. But for others, including serious crimes of violence like assault, robbery, and rape, it is a very large problem indeed. The "official" rates of these crimes are greatly affected by peoples' ability or willingness to report them, and, in some situations, that willingness may be very low.

This has historically been especially true for some crimes affecting women, notably rape and domestic violence in the home. For a variety of reasons, including the traditional tendency for criminal justice systems around the world to fail to take these crimes against women very seriously and the cultural support for male violence in some societies, women have often been reluctant to report them to the authorities (and in some societies, authorities have been reluctant to record them as crimes even if they do). In some parts of the world, particularly in developing countries, this is a problem of such magnitude that official police data on such crimes cannot be considered reliable at all. In a recent survey of violence against women in ten countries around the world, the World Health Organization (WHO) discovered that between 55 percent and 95 percent of abused women, depending on the site studied, had never gone to *any* authorities—including not just police but local and religious leaders and nongovernmental organizations as well—to report the violence (WHO, 2005, Ch. 5 p. 1). Even in the most advanced industrial societies, many women remain reluctant to report such crimes to the police—either because they don't think they will be taken seriously or because they fear retaliation on the part of their abuser, or, sometimes, because they do not want a partner, even an abusive one, to go to jail. A recent survey of sexual assault in Washington state found that only about 23 percent of young women who had been assaulted reported the event to police; among those who had been attacked when they were teenagers, only 8 percent reported it to police (Casey and Nurius, 2006).

As a result, statistics on those crimes are extraordinarily sensitive to changes in women's reporting practices. The Washington state survey found that the proportion of assaulted women who had reported the crime to police, although still startlingly low, had doubled from just 11 percent among older women in the survey to 23 percent among women who were younger, and thus had been assaulted more recently (Casey and Nurius, 2006). An example of this phenomenon from Latin America is particularly striking. In several countries—including Brazil, Costa Rica, Argentina, and Uruguay—special "women's police stations" were established in the 1980s, partly in order to help overcome women's reluctance to report crimes against them. One result was that in some places the official count of violence against women dramatically increased: in São Paulo, Brazil, reported cases of rape went from 67 in 1985—before a women's police station opened—to 841 in 1990 (Ayres, 1998).

Another problem with relying on crimes reported to police is that a great deal of violent crime is committed against people who are themselves either involved in crime or for some other reason are highly resistant to reporting it to authorities. In general, the young, the poor, and minorities report crime less often to the police. Even very serious crimes—like robberies and assaults—committed against young people involved in drug dealing or youth gangs are unlikely to come to the attention of the police. So many of the people most likely to be victims of violence rarely tell the police when it happens—which means that, as far as the statistics go, it did not happen. Obviously, that contributes to the tendency of these "official" statistics to understate the amount of violent crime. This problem may indeed be getting worse, because, as we'll see later, there is good reason to believe that serious violent crime is becoming increasingly concentrated among the groups who are already most vulnerable to it—especially the extremely disadvantaged and marginalized young.

These issues become especially troublesome when we're looking at changes in crime rates over time or trying to compare one country with another. In the United States, for example, changing laws and public attitudes toward domestic violence in the 1980s and 1990s led to many more women reporting these crimes. The result was a large increase in our reported rates of the crime of aggravated assault (which is what much violence against women in the home would be called if it were being taken seriously)—increases that represented only partly the real increases in violence, and partly an increased willingness on the part of the victims to report the crimes.

In many European countries after World War II, similarly, official police data showed large increases in some kinds of crime—including, in some places, assaults and robberies. This has led some to argue that sharp rises in violence were a common feature of most, if not all, advanced societies in the postwar era, an interpretation that turns out, on closer inspection, to be misleading. In many countries, these official increases reflected mainly an increased tendency for people to report crimes, and to expand the range of incidents that they defined as crimes worthy of being reported to authorities (Estrada, 2001, 2004; Junger-Tas, 2004).

Comparing police data across different countries is also difficult because one country's definition of a violent crime may not be the same as another country's. In England and Wales, for example, government uses the term *wounding* to describe assaults that result in injury—a concept that is similar, but not the same as, what in the United States is called *aggravated assault*. Even comparing homicide, the most serious and visible of violent crimes, across different countries—which might seem simple—is often more complicated in practice. In some countries, for example, but not others, police statistics on homicide include *attempted* murders as well as completed ones. Adding attempted killings naturally inflates the country's homicide rate, making it very difficult to compare it with the homicide rate in a country that doesn't count such failed attempts.

Finally, there is another problem, less common than it used to be and less common in advanced democracies than elsewhere, but still important, especially in the developing world and, to some extent, in the United States. In order for a crime to appear in police statistics, it must not only be reported to the police, but must also be honestly and accurately recorded by them when it is. The police, after all, have a stake in seeming to be effective in fighting crime, so there is a temptation to distort the statistics to make the situation look better than it is. Sometimes, for example, police may redefine serious crimes as more minor ones—a practice often known as *downgrading offenses*—or even fail to record them altogether.

This is still enough of a problem in the United States that crime statistics from some cities in recent years have had to be discarded because they were known to be misleading. In the former Soviet bloc, where authorities apparently systematically downplayed the extent of crime for decades, the problem was far worse—such that most criminologists believe that statistics from those countries must be treated with special caution. In China, according to one study, it's estimated that before the 1990s, "about one-third of the crimes were not reported from the local police units to the national police because local officials wanted to 'look better' in their efforts to secure social order" (Liu and Messner, 2004, p.14).

One response to the problems of police statistics was the development of the "victim survey" or "criminal victimization survey," in which a sample of the population is interviewed about their experiences with crime. These surveys, pioneered in the United States in the 1960s, have since been conducted in a number of other countries, particularly in Europe, and an international crime victim survey has been carried out every few years since the 1980s.

The principle here is simple and, at least on the surface, compelling. By asking people directly if they have been victims of crime, researchers avoid the fundamental problem of depending on people's willingness to report the incident to the police. Accordingly, the victim surveys should reveal a larger amount of crime than the police statistics do, and this turns out to be true. The victim surveys suggest that a great deal more crime is committed than we know from official figures—particularly some kinds of crime—and that most crimes, even fairly serious crimes of violence, are not reported to the police. (Note that victim surveys do not include the most serious crime of violence—homicide—for the obvious reason that the victim cannot be interviewed.)

Nevertheless, these surveys also sharply underestimate violent crime, particularly in some countries, for reasons that are less often acknowledged but are quite fundamental. Most importantly, it's clear that some of the same obstacles to reporting that distort police statistics also apply to the victim surveys. For example, because most such surveys (with some important exceptions) are done by telephone as part of what is called a "household" survey, they leave out people who don't have telephones; more crucially, they leave out people who do not have homes (see, e.g., Westfelt and Estrada, 2004). More generally, they tend to leave out people who don't want to talk about their involvement with violence. Historically, that was a very big problem with the figures for crimes against women in such surveys—rape and domestic violence—because, as with the police data, women who were victims of these crimes were reluctant to report them to authorities of any kind.

Less often considered, but extremely important, is that—again, as with police reports—a great deal of violent crime is committed against people who are involved in crime themselves, and who therefore are reluctant to talk about the circumstances with authorities, whether police or interviewers representing a government agency. People who are involved in drug dealing, for example, or in youth gangs or other ongoing criminal activities, are unlikely to be contacted in a victim survey to begin with, and even less likely to talk openly about their experience with crime if they are contacted. And that's especially problematic, because these are people whom we know have among the highest risks of being victims of violence. One recent study, for example, found that youth who had been in juvenile detention in Chicago were more than four times as likely to die—overwhelmingly by violence—as their counterparts in the city's general population (Teplin, McClelland, Abram, and Mileusnic, 2005).

In general, most victim surveys tend to undercount people who are socially and economically marginal—people who are very poor, people who are homeless, people who live in very disorganized communities or very troubled family situations, or who engage in dangerous illicit occupations like drug dealing or sex work. But, as we will see, it is precisely among these groups (along with delinquent youth) that the risk of being a victim of violent crime is the highest. In many such surveys there are attempts to statistically correct the problem of underrepresenting certain racial or ethnic minorities or the poor, but for the most part they do not effectively address the more specific issue of the exclusion of the most violence-prone groups. As a result, the surveys understate the overall level of crime, even serious violent crimes, in societies where there are a large proportion of people in those especially high-risk groups.

This point is driven home by research that has tried to determine the rate of violence among the kinds of people who are most often left out of conventional victim surveys. One recent study of victimization among homeless people in San Francisco, California, for example, found that fully one third of women and 27 percent of men reported having been physically or sexually assaulted in the past year. One half of the homeless people in the survey reported having been robbed at least once in the past year (Kushel, Evans, Perry, Robertson, and Moss, 2003). These rates of victimization are far higher than those in the general population—the most recent victim survey estimates an overall robbery rate of 2.6 per 1,000—and it is fair to say that the great majority of this routine violence is never picked up by standard victimization surveys (or, for that matter, by police statistics) (U.S. Bureau of Justice Statistics, 2006, p. 2). And with a homeless population in the United States that is variously estimated at between 700,000 and 2 million people at any given point, this is a very consequential omission.

The homeless are at especially high risk of being victims of violence for a number of reasons—partly because their lack of protective shelter makes them more vulnerable—they have "no door to lock," as the

San Francisco study (Kushel et al., 2003) puts it; partly, too, because they are likely to live in or near high crime areas and to engage in high-risk activities like prostitution, using and selling illicit drugs, and drinking heavily. One study found a homicide death rate of 242 per 100,000 among homeless men in Boston, a rate that is many times that of the male population as a whole (Hwang, Orav, O'Connell, Lebow, and Brennan, 1997). And the undercounting of violence among the homeless is only part of the larger tendency for victim surveys to miss much of the crime that takes place among the most severely disadvantaged parts of the population. As with the police statistics, this limitation is, if anything, becoming more troublesome as the most serious kinds of violence become increasingly concentrated in precisely those groups—an issue we will return to later.

Finally, victim surveys—like police data—also leave out people who are in institutions, including those who are locked up in jails and prisons. Once again, the great problem with this omission is that the kind of people who wind up in prison are far more likely than the population as a whole to be victims, as well as perpetrators, of crime; and that is true both while they're behind bars and while they are on the street. Therefore, to the extent that they are left out, victimization surveys seriously underestimate the amount of violence that actually takes place in a society.

In general, then, victimization surveys tend to be most accurate in uncovering the experience of crime among the relatively stable and trusting segments of the population. But their experience is only part of the overall picture of violence, and it is arguably not the most crucial part. Even among the people who are covered in victimization surveys, moreover, there are serious problems of reliability with these surveys. For example, the *response rate*—the numbers of people who actually take part in such surveys when they are called—is often extremely low (falling below 40 percent in some countries in international surveys, for example) and have been falling for many years (Westfelt and Estrada, 2004; Simon, Mercy, and Barker, 2006).

These limitations become especially troublesome when it comes to comparing victimization data across different societies. If these problems affected all countries equally, they would cause less trouble. But they do not. The proportion of the population that is not stable or trusting and is therefore likely to be missed by these surveys varies greatly across different countries—even within the developed industrial world[1]. We will look at this issue more closely later, when we explore the connections between inequality and violence. For now, it's important to note that the United States, among the advanced industrial societies of the world, has a much higher proportion of its population that is extremely poor, a much higher proportion that is homeless, and a much higher proportion that is behind bars. As a result, its victim surveys almost certainly miss a far greater proportion of serious violent crime than those of most other developed countries, thus making the United States "look better" comparatively than it really is.

Another approach to exploring the extent of violence within and between societies is through self-report surveys, in which samples of the population or of particular populations—such as high school students—are asked to report if and how often they have committed a crime or engaged in some other kind of illegal activity. These are not usually designed to estimate the level of crime in a society as a whole, as some victimization surveys are, but on a smaller scale they have been conducted in many countries, and there have been some efforts in

[1]There is also evidence that marginal groups in other advanced industrial societies, including the homeless, although they are at a higher risk of violence and other social problems than the general population in their countries, are nevertheless less likely to be victims than similar populations in the United States. One study of homeless people in Canada, for example, found that even though homeless men were much more likely to die of a variety of causes than other Canadians, they were much less likely to die of a number of causes, including violence, than their counterparts in the United States (Hwang, 2000).

recent years to do them in several countries at once. Self-report surveys suffer from the same sorts of difficulties as the victim surveys do—only more so. The basic problem is that because people are asked to acknowledge engaging in behavior that is illegal, there is likely to be considerable reluctance to tell the truth. That's not an abstract possibility: studies show, for example, that people are often less than honest in reporting their drug use in such surveys. And as is true of both police data and victim surveys, the problem of underreporting in self-report surveys is particularly troublesome among some groups. There is considerable evidence from several countries that young people from disadvantaged minority groups tend to underreport their involvement in crime and violence (see Oberwittler and Hofer, 2005, for some European examples). And because many self-report studies of youth crime are administered to students in schools, they often leave out young people who are not in school—notably school dropouts—whose risks of violence are likely to be the highest.

These caveats don't mean that self-report studies have nothing to tell us. Like the victim surveys, these studies do show that there is a great deal more crime in many societies than the official statistics on crimes reported to the police suggest. But the limits of these surveys, especially when comparing crime across social divisions or across countries, are serious—more so than some researchers have been willing to acknowledge.

Medical care systems around the world furnish two further kinds of data that are especially useful in understanding patterns of violence: statistics of *mortality*—that is, statistics on the causes of death, including deaths by violence; and statistics on the number of people who go to hospitals because of a violence-related injury. Studies based on the data from hospitals, unfortunately, are relatively rare and available only for some countries, including the United States. Yet they are revealing, in part because they show once again the limits of other measures of violent crime. In the United States, emergency room statistics turn up approximately three times the rate of serious violent assaults as the victim surveys do—which, in turn, as we've seen, report far higher rates of violent crime than is reported to the police. The hospital figures are higher because people who are seriously injured are likely to seek medical help—even if they would be unwilling to report the crime to the police (or to a government interviewer over the telephone), assuming they were contacted in the first place. Sometimes, to be sure, people go to extraordinary lengths to hide their injuries from anyone, including the medical system, particularly if they were injured in the course of doing something illegal themselves, or if they simply don't trust the medical, or any other, authorities. In some urban communities in the United States, for example, even stabbing or gunshot victims may refuse to go to the hospital, opting to treat themselves, or have family or friends patch them up, instead. But, it is a good bet that when it comes to the most serious incidents, these statistics get us closer to the real rate of violence.

The data on mortality—deaths from violence—are even stronger. They are widely considered to be the most accurate evidence we have, and as a result they are what researchers most often use to study violence comparatively across different societies. They are not perfect: Even in the most advanced societies with the best health care systems and the most reliable medical records, not every killing is accurately counted as such. In some poorer or more volatile countries, this is a much more severe problem, because their medical care systems are insufficiently developed to do a reliable job of collecting and reporting information on deaths. At the extreme, those systems may be disrupted by war or social upheaval. In addition, of course, mortality data only tell us about people who die from violence—leaving out the vastly greater number who are injured but survive. The WHO estimates, for example, that for every fatal assault in Europe, there are 20 to 40 non-fatal but serious ones (Sethi, Racioppi, Baumgarten, and Vida, 2005, p. 28). In the United States, it's estimated that there are more than 1.6 million hospital admissions for violent injuries each year, but only 16,000 to 25,000 homicides (Centers for Disease Control [CDC], 2007).

But, although these data are far from perfect, they have two great advantages. First, homicide is hard to hide, or to call something else, especially in developed countries—and medical authorities, unlike police, usually have no reason to want to distort the data. Second, we have an international organization—the WHO, which is part of the United Nations—that has collected data from health authorities around the world for many years, and imposes a common definition of homicide on all of the reporting countries. As a result, the statistics avoid the problem that bedevils official police statistics of having to deal with varying legal definitions of crime.

Do these relatively reliable homicide statistics give us an indication of the extent of other forms of violence? That is, does the level of homicide tend to correspond to that of nonfatal assaults, sexual assaults, or robberies? That's a hard question to answer, because it's so difficult to get an accurate count of nonfatal violence. But the evidence suggests that homicide fits the broader pattern of violence in a given country more often than not. Societies wracked by killings are likely to be wracked by assaults and robberies as well, and vice-versa—although there are some important exceptions. That isn't surprising; after all, homicide could hardly be unrelated to other forms of violence. The difference between a homicide and an assault may hinge on whether someone shot their victim accurately or a knife glanced off a bone rather than hitting a vital organ, or the ambulance arrived quickly enough to get the victim to a hospital. There is no bright line, in other words, between fatal and nonfatal violence, and so it's reasonable to believe that a country with a high rate of homicide will have high rates of other kinds of violence as well.

(We'll see, however, there are some countries where a relatively high level of violence overall goes hand-in-hand with a relatively low rate of fatal violence. Why that should be true is complicated—and we'll look at some possible reasons).

To sum up the discussion so far: Although the issues surrounding the measurement of violent crime—especially across different societies—are complex, we can come to some basic conclusions. With the exception of the data on homicide, the most common measures of crime tend to underestimate—often quite severely—the true level of violence in modern societies, some of them more than others. They also certainly, as a result, minimize the gap in violence between the most dangerous countries and those that are less so.

There is another problem—more subtle, but increasingly important. It has to do with how we define the *crime rate* in the first place. The issue becomes particularly important if we want to compare crime between countries that have very large numbers of criminals behind bars and those that do not. The problem is that once someone who has committed a crime is locked away where they cannot commit more crimes—at least on the outside—they cease to be counted as part of that society's crime statistics. We measure the crime problem only by the activities of the criminals who remain free in the community—that's what we call the *crime rate*. But we badly distort our understanding of violent crime—and of our society's tendency to produce violent people—if we leave those offenders behind bars out of the equation.

A hypothetical example illustrates the problem. Suppose we are talking about illness, rather than violent crime. And suppose that in our society there is an epidemic of some very serious disease—say, cholera—that has devastated the population, killing many people and requiring us to put many others in hospitals. Now suppose we want to count the number of sick people—so that, among other things, we can come up with ways of understanding where the disease is most prevalent and how we could prevent it. Would we leave the people we have put in the hospitals out of the count of those who are sick? Of course not; they are not only an important part of the problem, but arguably the most severe part of it—the sickest among the victims of the disease. So we must certainly count all of the sick, both the institutionalized and those still living in the community.

But we don't do that when we measure crime, because we don't measure the number of criminals we have produced, but only the number of crimes (or some of them) that those criminals commit while they are in the community. Unlike the sick people in hospitals, the violent people in prisons are not counted as part of our crime problem. But they *are* part of the problem. They don't cease being products of whatever it is about our society that creates criminals just because we've moved them—hidden them both from sight and from our crime statistics.

This may sound numbingly technical, but it is actually very important—especially in understanding one society's propensity to breed violent crime as compared with others. Suppose we have two countries, both of which have roughly the same level of violent crime—the same rate of robberies, assaults, rapes, and murders. But one country also has ten times as many violent offenders, proportionately, behind bars as the other. Do the two countries have the same crime problem? Hardly—because one country has the same amount of violent crime despite having already put away great numbers of criminals. Even having taken many of its worst offenders off the streets, in other words, that country is still plagued by violence. The troubling combination of high violent crime and high incarceration tells us that things are in worse shape than we would know by looking at the crime rate alone; and if we simply compared the crime problem in the two countries on the basis of their measured crime rates, we would miss that crucial dimension altogether.

Again, this may sound abstract, but it is very important in comparing countries like the United States or Russia with other countries that incarcerate a far smaller proportion of the population. As we will see, the United States and Russia have very high crime even if we ignore the implication of those enormous prison populations. Yet factoring in those hidden criminals tells us that the problem is even more serious than we usually acknowledge—and the differences with other, less violent countries even greater (for a fuller discussion of this point, see Currie, 2003).

With that in mind, let's take a look at what we know from our admittedly limited data about violence around the world—beginning with what the mortality data tell us about the risks of dying by violence.

B. THE DIFFERENT WORLDS OF VIOLENCE

As I've said, what is most startling about violent death around the world today is its variability. In many countries, the chance that someone will be deliberately killed by another person is tiny. In others it is a very real possibility, an inescapable, harsh fact of life—especially for some groups in the population. And on the whole, these patterns turn out to be fairly predictable. The stratification of the risk of violent death goes along with other disadvantages. Overall, with one stunning exception, it is poor- or middle-income countries that suffer the highest risks of fatal violence. Nations that are better off in other ways are better off in this respect as well. And the differences are truly extreme, as Chart 1, based on WHO mortality statistics, shows.

The figures are for various years around the turn of the twenty-first century. They describe the number of deaths by homicide, expressed as a proportion—the number per 100,000 overall population, a strategy used

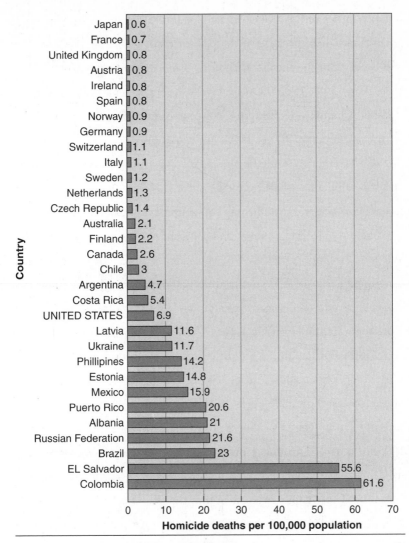

Country	Homicide deaths per 100,000 population
Japan	0.6
France	0.7
United Kingdom	0.8
Austria	0.8
Ireland	0.8
Spain	0.8
Norway	0.9
Germany	0.9
Switzerland	1.1
Italy	1.1
Sweden	1.2
Netherlands	1.3
Czech Republic	1.4
Australia	2.1
Finland	2.2
Canada	2.6
Chile	3
Argentina	4.7
Costa Rica	5.4
UNITED STATES	6.9
Latvia	11.6
Ukraine	11.7
Phillipines	14.2
Estonia	14.8
Mexico	15.9
Puerto Rico	20.6
Albania	21
Russian Federation	21.6
Brazil	23
EL Salvador	55.6
Colombia	61.6

CHART 1 HOMICIDE DEATH RATES, SELECTED COUNTRIES

to control for the different population sizes in different countries. Other things being equal, more people will die of homicide in a country with a bigger population than in a country with a smaller one. So standardizing the rate by looking at the number who die per 100,000 population allows us to compare the likelihood of violence across countries of different sizes.

That likelihood differs enormously across the countries in the chart. At one extreme are some Latin American countries, closely followed by some countries of the former Soviet bloc (and some in Africa, which are not included here because of the lack of comparable data). Colombia and El Salvador top the list, with rates of more than 60 per 100,000 and more than 55 per 100,000, respectively. Several other countries—Brazil, Russia, Albania, and Puerto Rico—come in with rates of homicide deaths of more than 20 per 100,000 population.

At the other extreme, a number of countries—mostly in Europe and a few in Asia—had homicide rates less than 1 per 100,000. In recent years both large and small countries have enjoyed homicide rates at or below that level at some point, including Austria, Japan, France, Sweden, Ireland, Greece, Norway, Switzerland, and the United Kingdom. The risk of violent death in Colombia at the time these statistics were gathered was approximately 88 times that in France and more than 100 times that in Japan.

Within Europe alone, the differences are astonishing. As a recent WHO report points out, Europe has both some of the highest and some of the lowest homicide rates in the modern world—ranging most recently from Russia's 24 per 100,000 and Kazakhstan's 15 per 100,000 down to around 1 per 100,000 in Sweden, Switzerland, and the United Kingdom, and well below 1 per 100,000 in Austria and Germany. These gaps are so stark that the WHO calculates that if the overall European rates of homicide were brought down to the level of the country with the lowest rate, 87 percent of all homicides in Europe would be prevented—or a total of 55,000 lives saved every year (Sethi, Racioppi, Baumgarten, and Vida, 2005). (Note that these more recent figures are slightly different from those in Chart 1.)

So the differences in the risks of homicide are huge—so large, in fact, that they trump other factors that usually are decisive in shaping the likelihood of being a victim of violence. One of those factors is gender. Around the world, men are generally more likely to die by violence than women—about four times as likely, for example, in Russia. But a Russian woman in the year 2004 was nearly 13 times as likely to die by violence as a French *man* and 17 times as likely as a German man.[2]

For the most part, the global distribution of violent death falls along fairly predictable lines of wealth and development. All of the very low violence countries in Chart 1 are advanced, affluent industrial societies—although as we will see, some low-violence countries are considerably less affluent than others. The high-violence countries, however, are almost always found at the lower to middle end of the scale of affluence and economic development. Within Europe, the risk of violent death is 15 times higher in the low- to middle-income countries (including Russia and some other former Soviet countries) than it is in higher-income ones (Krug et al., 2002, p. 274).

These sharp divisions translate into great differences in the extent to which violence contributes to the overall risk of dying in a country's population. In the higher-income countries of Europe, including countries like Germany, France, the United Kingdom, and Sweden, homicide accounts for only a small proportion of all deaths—roughly 1 in 1000—and it ranks 44th on the list of leading causes of death. In the low- and middle-income countries of North, South, and Central America, however, homicide accounts for 1 in 22 deaths, and is the fifth leading cause of death overall, trailing only heart disease, stroke, respiratory infections, and diabetes (Krug et al., 2002, pp. 291, 295).

There is one startling exception to the general rule that richer countries are safer countries, and that is the United States. Its homicide rate in recent years of around 6 per 100,000 does not put it with the worst countries in Latin America and the Caribbean, or the former Soviet

[2]Interestingly, these gender differences tend to be wider in countries with high levels of violence overall. In Russia and the United States, the risk premium for being a man is four times that of a woman; in Switzerland, the difference in homicide risk between men and women practically disappears.

Union, but it does make the United States stand out very starkly among the rest of the world's developed countries. That rate means that the chances of dying by violence in the United States range from roughly 4 to more than 10 times those of most of the other rich countries of the world. To put this difference more starkly, in 2006, there were more deaths from homicide in Oakland, California—a city of about 375,000 people—than in the entire country of Sweden, with a population of almost 9 million.

Indeed, the United States' homicide death rate puts us above some of the countries of the developing world—including Chile, Costa Rica, and Argentina. Using the WHO's hypothetical exercise, if the United States had the homicide rate of the average European high-income country—about 1 per 100,000—we would avoid 5 out of every 6 of our homicides, thus saving more than 13,000 American lives every year, or more than four times the number who died in the terrorist attacks of September 11, 2001.

The anomaly of the United States' level of violence is even more striking if we focus on the group at greatest risk—young men. The predominance of young males as victims of violent deaths is a highly visible feature in many—although not all—of the societies most wracked by violence. (In Russia, among other countries, it's men in their 30s who have the highest rates of violent death.) In some parts of Latin America, for example, the rates of violent death for men ages 15 to 29 are astonishing: 37 per 100,000 in Mexico, 64 per 100,000 in Venezuela, 80 per 100,000 in Brazil, 100 per 100,000 in Puerto Rico, 133 per 100,000 in El Salvador, and more than 200 per 100,000 in Colombia (WHO, 2002).[3] In some districts in the city of São Paulo, Brazil, the homicide death rate for young men this age is more than 400 per 100,000

[3]The rates in Colombia have fallen somewhat more recently.

(CDC, 2004). At the same time, there are some countries with generally low violence rates in which young men are not particularly more likely than other people to be the victims of homicide. As a result, the comparative risks of death for young men in different places in the world can be even greater than for the population as a whole, and indeed truly mind-boggling. A young man in Puerto Rico is more than 100 times more likely to die by violence than a youth in France, and 200 times more likely than a youth the same age in Japan.

Among the rich countries of the world, the United States comes closer, in this respect, to the pattern that is usually found in some of the poorer countries; its level of youth violence more closely resembles that of some Third World countries than it does the rest of the advanced world. The American rate of homicide death for young males ages 15 to 29—more than 20 per 100,000 during the last several years—puts the United States in the close company of such countries as Paraguay, Kazakhstan, and Trinidad and Tobago.

Once again, this difference overrides the usual gender patterns. An American female ages 15 to 29 is three times more likely to be murdered as an English male, nearly five times as likely as a French male, and nine times as likely as a Japanese male.

These numbers may seem abstract and cold on the surface, but they reflect sharp differences in the quality of life for youth across these different worlds of violence. In the United States, as in Latin America, violence is a leading cause of death for young people, and young men in particular. In many of the other affluent societies around the world it is a rare event. It simply is not a fact of ordinary life for young men in Copenhagen, Tokyo, Stockholm, or, for that matter, Toronto. For the young men of San Salvador, São Paulo, Moscow, or Baltimore, it is.

In Canada, Germany, and Switzerland, about 1 adolescent male death in 65 is the result of violence. In France, it's 1 in 74. In Japan, it's

1 in 114. But in Russia, better than 1 in 10 young men who die of any cause die of homicide. In the United States and Mexico, more than 1 in 5 adolescent male deaths is the result of violence; in Brazil, it is 1 in 2.4.

The sharp differences between the United States and other advanced societies, moreover, remain even after the much-celebrated fall in crime in American crime rates during the 1990s. The decline in crime in those years—roughly 1994 to 2000—was very significant, but it must be seen in context. American homicide rates fell from their peaks in the early 1980s and 1990s, when they reached close to 10 per 100,000, but they remained higher than they were a generation earlier, and, most importantly, the decline did not come close to closing the gap between the United States and the rest of the developed world in the risks of dying by violence. (It's especially important to keep this in mind because, as I discuss later, many countries have lately been moving to copy American approaches to combating crime, including countries whose levels of serious violent crime are far lower than ours.)

These differences show up very early. Violent death is always tragic, but especially so when the victims are children. The data we have on killings of young children (usually at the hands of parents or other caretakers) are less trustworthy than they are for older youth and adults. It is sometimes difficult to distinguish child homicides from accidental deaths, and it is only in the countries of the advanced industrial world, on the whole, that the infrastructure to record these deaths is sufficiently developed—countries with the most advanced health-care systems and the greatest official sensitivity to violence behind closed doors. But the broad picture is clear, and deeply troubling.

In general, the pattern of child deaths by violence fits that for older people, with low rates in most advanced industrial societies and higher rates in such places as the former Soviet Union, the Third World, and the United States. But the situation in the United States, according to the mortality statistics, is especially striking. Among male children ages from birth through age 4, the rate of violent death in the United States is the highest recorded in the WHO statistics; significantly higher than in such other high violence countries as Russia, Ukraine, Mexico, Brazil, and even Colombia—and roughly four times that of the United Kingdom or Japan. A number of countries had so few recorded child homicide deaths that the WHO did not calculate a rate for them. A few—including Israel, Italy, and Sweden—registered zero violent deaths of male children this age in the most recent year covered by the data (Krug et al., 2002). Again, these figures must be viewed carefully, and they cannot be considered precise, but the broad pattern—the relatively low incidence of fatal child abuse in most advanced industrial societies and the startlingly high level in the United States—is impossible to ignore.

Again, child abuse, by its nature, is a difficult crime to prove, and we know that even fatal cases may fly under the radar of health authorities (and police), and therefore not get counted in mortality statistics. Yet that is likely to be more true in some of the high-violence countries than in the low-violence countries of, say, Western Europe—which means that, if anything, these disparities may be even greater than the figures suggest. The killing of an infant or toddler is more likely to be investigated and recorded as such in Sweden or Canada than it is in the Ukraine, or, for that matter, in parts of the United States. Accordingly, the situation for very young children in the latter countries may be even worse than the already stunning statistics suggest.

It's important to realize that when we talk about differences between countries' levels of violence, we are painting with a very broad brush and obscuring important variations within the countries themselves. That's especially true in the case of the United States. When we speak of "American" levels of violence, we are actually mixing together very different experiences in different states and regions. Some

American states—in the Midwest and in New England—have homicide rates that are not so different from many countries of affluent Europe. Others, especially in the South, have rates that come even closer to matching those of some of the most dangerous countries of the Third World. Maine, Vermont, Iowa, New Hampshire, and North Dakota all had homicide death rates of less than 2 per 100,000 in 2004. Louisiana, however, had a rate of about 13 per 100,000, more than double that of the United States as a whole and eight times that of the state with the lowest rate—Maine. If the United States as a whole enjoyed Maine's homicide death rate in 2004, more than 12,500 Americans would have lived who actually died by violence; about 73 percent of homicides across the country would have been averted (CDC, 2007).

There are similar, although less stark, patterns in countries outside the United States. In the United Kingdom, for example, young men die of violence five times as often, proportionately, in Scotland as in England. Scotland's rate of youth homicide deaths, low by American standards at around 7 per 100,000, makes Scotland by far the most dangerous country, when it comes to youth violence, among the high-income countries of Europe (Krug et al., 2002).

So far, we have been looking at these international variations as they play out today, in the twenty-first century. But it is important to understand that they have been with us, in strikingly similar form, for at least half a century. In the last half of the twentieth century, the United States' homicide rate never dropped much below 5 per 100,000. The average rate during that half-century was about 7.5 per 100,000, and the highest was 10.5 per 100,000. Meanwhile, several countries averaged a homicide death rate of less than 1 per 100,000 across the entire 50-year period—including Denmark, France, Iceland, Ireland, the Netherlands, Norway, Spain, and the United Kingdom. Other countries averaged only a little higher, right around 1 per 100,000: Sweden, Switzerland,

Portugal, New Zealand, Japan, Israel, Greece, Germany, Belgium, and Austria. Several of these countries (over somewhat varying periods) never had an annual homicide rate higher than 2 per 100,000 during that time, or less than one fifth of the maximum and considerably less than one half of the minimum rate in the United States. That includes Austria, Denmark, France, Germany, the Netherlands, Norway, Portugal, Spain, Sweden, and the United Kingdom.

This list of the low homicide countries includes many of the advanced Western European countries as well as Japan. Notably, it includes some European countries that were relatively poor, compared to other Western European countries or the United States, during most of this period—Spain, Portugal, Ireland, and Greece. The *maximum* homicide rate in Spain was about one fourth of the *minimum* rate in the United States during the last half of the twentieth century.

Indeed, this difference carries over to a few countries of the developing world. Costa Rica's average homicide death rate was less than the United States' minimum rate for the last 50 years of the twentieth century, and far less than our average. Chile's average, at a little over 3 per 100,000, was also significantly below the U.S. minimum rate; their highest rate—at 6.6 per 100,000—was less than two thirds of the United States.

The countries that surpassed the United States in this grim statistic throughout the latter half of the twentieth century—as today—are a mixed group. Some of them are in Asia, including Thailand and the Philippines; some are in Latin America, including Mexico, Colombia, Venezuela and El Salvador; and some in the former Soviet bloc, including Estonia (LaFree & Tseloni, 2006).

So the sharp stratification of violent death across the world's countries has been with us for a long time; if anything, it has increased in recent years, so that we are now seeing an even more pronounced pulling away of the high-violence countries from the rest. In the former Soviet Union, for example, violent crime rocketed upward in the 1990s (Galinsky, 2006; Karstedt, 2003). In Latin America and the Caribbean, already high levels of violence similarly shot upward during the 1980s and 1990s, making them the highest of any region in the world (Ayres, 1998). In the United States, dramatic rises from a very high historical base, concentrated among young people, began in the 1960s and have waxed and waned since, but reached stunning peaks in the early 1990s despite massive efforts to "get tough" on violent crime and a vast increase in the country's prison population (Currie, 1998). Meanwhile, most of the countries with historically low rates of violent death have remained low—which, again, includes every other high-income, advanced industrial society besides the United States. In some of those countries, rates of homicide increased, particularly during the 1960s and 1970s, but they increased from a very low base level, and never rose to anything close to that in the United States or the other high-violence countries around the world. The result is an increasing social stratification of deadly violence, in which many—although not all—of the world's poorer nations bear the great bulk of the world's burden of killing, along with one wealthy society, the United States.

Does the pattern for homicide hold for other kinds of violent crime? This question is important, because although homicide is surely the worst of violent crimes, it is fortunately a very small part of the total of serious violence around the world.

Unfortunately, for reasons we touched on previously, it is harder to get a reliable picture of the extent of nonfatal violence, even within a single country, much less to compare them. We are forced to rely on measures that are usually profoundly limited and that certainly underestimate the amount of violence, especially in those places where it is likely to be worst. But the evidence we have suggests that homicide is not an isolated problem. As we might expect, places where people are likely to die at the hands of others are also places where they are likely to be injured, robbed, or sexually assaulted. The fit is imperfect, and there are some important exceptions, which may in themselves tell us important things about the sources of violence. Overall, however, there is a congruence between fatal and nonfatal forms of violence, no matter what method we use to study it.

We know, for example, that nonfatal gun assaults are very common in the United States (and in some other high-violence countries, including some in Latin America), but very uncommon in most other advanced industrial societies. In the United States there are roughly four nonfatal gun assault injuries treated in hospital emergency rooms for every gunshot homicide—which translates into a minimum of more than 50,000 nonfatal gun attacks every year, or about 137 every day (CDC, 2007). Nothing comparable happens, as we'll see, in any of the low-violence countries of Europe, East Asia, Canada, or the Pacific.

International victim survey data, even though they are limited in the ways I've described, likewise show that on the whole, countries with high levels of violent death also have high levels of nonfatal violence. Again, that's especially significant because we know that victim surveys minimize the extent and seriousness of violence, especially in some of the countries that suffer it the most. One recent study of victimization data for 27 countries—including most of the high-income countries of Western Europe along with several Eastern European countries, Japan, Canada, the United States, Australia, and New Zealand—found that, on average, the Eastern European countries have higher levels of assault and robbery than their Western European or

Asian counterparts, just as they do for homicide. The country with the highest proportion of people reporting having been assaulted or robbed—Estonia—had a rate 16 times that of the country with the lowest—Japan. The United States scored number three on this list out of 27 countries, after Estonia and New Zealand—higher than such countries as Lithuania and Poland. The U.S. rates of robbery and assault combined were about twice those of Switzerland, 2.5 times those of Austria, about 3 times those in Italy or Portugal, and startlingly, 12 times higher than those in Japan (Van Wilsem, 2004). Again, these differences—large enough in themselves—almost certainly underestimate the real gaps between the United States and these other advanced industrial societies, because of the larger "dark figure" haunting victim surveys in the United States—the fact that a greater proportion of the people with very high risks of victimization are left out of the count.

Generally, the 27 countries ranked fairly similarly on both homicide and other forms of violent crime. The United States came in third on both; Germany was number 23 on homicide and number 20 on robbery and assault; Austria, 21 and 24; and Estonia topped the list at number 1 on both homicide deaths and victim-reported robberies and assaults (keep in mind that the study included only 27 countries, meaning that many others at both ends of the spectrum of violence were left out).

There are some interesting exceptions to that overall congruence. The United Kingdom, for example, ranks almost at the bottom in homicide rates among these countries, beaten only by Japan for the lowest spot in the list, but it ranks ninth on assault and robbery—suggesting, although we don't know for sure without more reliable evidence, that something may be keeping the British homicide rate low despite levels of other violence that are noticeably higher than the average among advanced industrial countries. (We'll return to this issue shortly.)

Measured this way, the variation among countries in rates of assault and robbery isn't as wide as it is for lethal violence, although the broad *ranking* of the countries is similar. Why the difference? We don't know for sure, but it most likely reflects both the limits of this kind of data, which again probably understate the disparities in nonlethal violence, and wider real gaps in homicide. The United States in particular would surely show even wider disparities with other countries in nonfatal violence if we were not relying on victim surveys that exclude many of the most frequently victimized people. However, there are also aspects of violence in America—notably the extraordinary prevalence of guns—that make fatal violence especially likely in the United States as compared with many other advanced industrial societies. We'll consider that issue in more detail in a moment.

It is even more difficult to compare levels of *domestic* violence across different countries, because it is so often hidden and because what is and is not considered unacceptable violence among intimate partners varies greatly around the world. But a careful study of women in 10 countries by the WHO (2005) tried to overcome some of those obstacles. This was a victim survey, but an unusually well-designed and thoughtful one. It used a variety of strategies to address the problem of women's reluctance to talk about abuse, including using only female interviewers who were carefully selected and trained to be sensitive and empathic. As the study's authors point out, this didn't eliminate the difficulties, but it does provide the best comparative evidence we have so far on patterns of domestic violence.

Once again, what is most striking about their results is the extraordinary variation in the risks women face. The researchers interviewed women at 15 sites in 10 countries. Some of the sites were urban, others what the researchers called *provincial*, mixing some rural and, often, some smaller urban settings. It asked about both physical and sexual violence, and within the category of physical violence, it distinguished between *severe* violence—including being hit with a fist, kicked, dragged, threatened with a weapon, or actually having one used against them—and *moderate* violence, including being slapped, shoved, or pushed. The chances of a woman having ever been the victim of any kind of physical or sexual violence by an intimate partner ranged from 15 percent in urban Japan to 71 percent in provincial Ethiopia. The chance of having ever been the victim of *severe* physical violence ranged from 4 percent in Japan to 49 percent in rural Peru. In between were, for example, women in Tanzania and Samoa (about 25 percent); urban Brazil (16 percent); and urban Serbia and Montenegro, in the former Yugoslavia (8 percent). Translated into the relative risks of being the victim of severe violence by an intimate partner, this means that a woman in rural Peru was about 12 times as likely to be attacked as her counterpart in urban Japan; a Samoan woman, 6 times as likely. The lesson is clear: "The wide variation in prevalence rates signals that this violence is not inevitable" (WHO, 2005, Ch. 2, p. 1).

Other kinds of evidence also support the great diversity of the experience of violence—both fatal and nonfatal—across different countries. Violence by youth gangs, for example, bedevils the United States (and some developing countries), to a degree that is unmatched in the rest of the developed world. One recent review of studies of street gangs in Europe concludes that although gangs do appear in many affluent European countries, and are involved in a disproportionate amount of violence, the level of violence associated with gangs is nowhere near what is routinely found in the United States (Klein, Weerman, and Thornberry, 2006). The gang problem may be growing in some countries, along with adverse social changes that are bringing them closer to the United States in important ways. But it remains true that outside of the United States and some of the countries of the developing world, cities are simply not plagued by the routine drive-by shootings that torment some American neighborhoods.

Let me be clear: No society in the contemporary world is free from violence, and none have been immune from tragedies and needless deaths. I don't mean to romanticize the situation in other advanced industrial societies. In some of them, violent crime, although less severe than in the United States, is nevertheless a nagging problem. In most, a great deal of family violence goes on behind closed doors and never comes to light. In some, too, there have been significant increases in violence in recent years. The impact of these problems on the quality of life should nowhere be trivialized.

But the bottom line is that violence is far more serious, pervasive, and devastating in some places than others—and overall, those disparities are increasing, not diminishing. Now the question is, why should that be? What is it about some societies that places people who live in them at so much higher risk of being injured or killed by others?

II | EXPLANATIONS

There has been no shortage of explanations for the wide variation in crime across different societies, but only some of them actually fit the evidence. Others may be perennially popular, but fall apart on closer inspection. Let's look first at some common explanations that fail the test, and then at several that show more promise.

1. EXPLANATIONS THAT DON'T WORK

A. GENES

For more than a hundred years, particularly in the United States, it has been popular, off and on, to seek the causes of violent crime in the realm of biology. Today, the idea that the roots of crime are "in the genes" has once again become fashionable, especially in the mass media, where we often read that practically every aspect of our behavior—from our sexual preferences to our propensity to break the law—is determined by our DNA.

It's clear, however, that this sort of explanation fails when confronted with the enormous variation in serious violent crime. Unless you can show that there is some biological peculiarity or genetic defect that correlates with the different levels of violent crime in different societies, you cannot explain that variation on the basis of some sort of innate biological predisposition. And no one has ever shown credibly that such an individual biological characteristic exists—one that explains why so many more people are murdered in, say, Russia or El Salvador than in Finland or Costa Rica. The great variation in crime across different societies, indeed, is one of the most powerful arguments against these simplistic biological views.

This is not to say that everyone is equal in their physical or mental capacities, or that differences in those capacities—say, in cognitive ability—might not have some relation to their risks of crime, especially when combined with adverse social conditions. But the search for some kind of "violence gene," or some innate propensity that can account for variations in violent crime between societies, has proved fruitless.

In the past, it was often argued that differences in crime between societies (and within them) reflected innate racial or ethnic characteristics. In the United States, particularly in the early part of the twentieth century, it was common to say that crime, along with many other social ills, could be blamed on the inherent genetic deficiencies of some racial or nationality or ethnic groups, which, at that time, were said to include Eastern and Southern Europeans, people of African descent, Mexicans, Irish, and Jews. That kind of argument was refuted again and again from the 1930s onward, and is less often heard today. Yet similar views have a way of reemerging from time to time—not so much among scholars, but on the fringes of serious debate.

But even the most cursory look around the world shows the most fundamental problem with this "explanation": High levels of violent crime—and low levels of violent crime—can be found among people of all races. There are some mostly black countries—including South Africa, Haiti, and Jamaica—with very high rates of violent crime. There are others—including some of the islands of the French West Indies—where the rate of violent crime, particularly homicide, is strikingly low in comparison with other countries in the developing world. There are mostly white countries—including Russia and the Baltic countries—with levels of violent crime that are among the highest in the world, while virtually next door in Scandinavia are other mostly white countries with among the lowest rates of violent crime in the world. Among mainly Hispanic societies, homicide rates similarly range from some of the highest in the world—in places like El Salvador, Guatemala, and Colombia—to those in countries like Uruguay, Costa Rica, or Chile (not to mention Spain, which is even lower)—that are lower than the rate in the United States.

This is not to say that race is unimportant in understanding patterns of violent crime. As we'll see later, it is very important indeed in some societies—but not in the way these discredited biological theories suggest. In many countries, being a member of a racial or ethnic minority group means being disproportionately subject to a host of social and economic disadvantages that are closely linked to violent crime. But the evidence is clear that it is how people of different races are treated—not some innate biological qualities that set them off from others—that is relevant in understanding the roots of violence.

B. LENIENCY

Probably the most common explanation for the crime problem is that society is insufficiently tough on criminals—that we don't punish them severely enough, or consistently enough, to ensure that crime doesn't pay. That assumption can be found regularly in the newspapers of countries around the world, and it has helped many a politician get elected. But it, too, fails the comparative test.

If being too lenient with criminals explained why some countries were more violent than others, it would follow that those countries with lower crime rates must be more severe in their punishment of crimes, and those with higher rates must punish people more lightly; but the reality is the opposite.

I've said that there is wide variation across countries in the level of violence, but equally striking is the wide variation in punishment. Some countries maintain vast prison systems that consume a substantial share of social resources and confine a significant proportion of their population; in others, prisons are relatively few and the number of people in them very small. And in this respect, the argument has it backward: Among modern societies, high levels of violent crime and a punitive approach to lawbreaking often go hand in hand. The two most violent of the highly industrialized nations—the United States and Russia—also have the highest and second-highest proportions, respectively, of their population behind bars of all of the major countries of the world.

A less punitive attitude toward crime, in contrast, often goes hand in hand with very low rates of violence. Comparing countries on the extent to which they put offenders behind bars is complicated, in part because some countries that use prisons sparingly also put substantial numbers of offenders in closed psychiatric institutions, which may skew our understanding of how tolerant those countries really are (Pitts and Kuula 2006). Nevertheless, the big picture remains: On the whole, a "softer" and more constructive approach to crime is not only compatible with low violent crime, but may indeed be closely linked to it, even a precondition for it. As we'll see later, there is good reason to believe that beyond a certain point, punishment, if too severe, backfires—becoming part of the crime problem, not part of the solution. At the same time, there is also good reason to believe that treating offenders well is an important step in reducing the kind of alienation and social inequality that breeds violence.

A look at Chart 2 bears out these connections. Measured by what we call the *incarceration rate*—that is, the proportion of the population locked behind bars in prisons and jails at any given point—the United

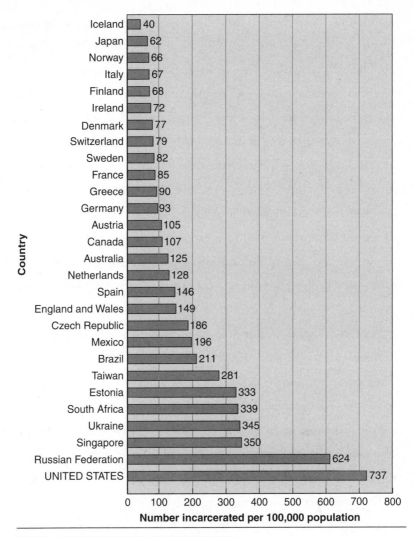

Country	
Iceland	40
Japan	62
Norway	66
Italy	67
Finland	68
Ireland	72
Denmark	77
Switzerland	79
Sweden	82
France	85
Greece	90
Germany	93
Austria	105
Canada	107
Australia	125
Netherlands	128
Spain	146
England and Wales	149
Czech Republic	186
Mexico	196
Brazil	211
Taiwan	281
Estonia	333
South Africa	339
Ukraine	345
Singapore	350
Russian Federation	624
UNITED STATES	737

Number incarcerated per 100,000 population

CHART 2 INCARCERATION RATES, SELECTED COUNTRIES

States, again, stands out most unusually on the list, particularly in comparison with the other affluent industrial societies of Europe, North America, Asia, and the Pacific.

The incarceration rate in the United States is well over 700 per 100,000 population. Again, that number doesn't mean much at first glance—until we realize that it is twelve times the proportion in Japan and more than ten times that of some European countries, including

Finland, Italy, and Ireland. Across the border to the north, Canada has an incarceration rate of 107 per 100,000, almost exactly one seventh of ours. These differences are not just significant—they are enormous. The Western European country with the highest rate of incarceration today is the United Kingdom, but its rate is about one fifth that of the United States—which is also true of its homicide rate. (It should be noted also that the United States is one of the only advanced industrial societies that still uses the death penalty against violent criminals—it has long since been abolished in all of the affluent countries of Western Europe, and indeed, in most of the lower-crime nations around the world.) Interestingly, the country with the next highest rate of imprisonment is Russia—which, as we've seen, is a country whose rate of violent crime is even higher than that of the United States.

In short, countries with high levels of violent crime tend to be those that punish more, not less. And this is not simply because high rates of serious crime necessarily lead to a large number of people being put behind bars. That is certainly part of the equation. But it's also true that these societies—the United States in particular—tend to sentence people to prison more often, for less-serious crimes, and to sentence them for longer terms than do comparable countries with lower crime rates (Currie 1998).

These differences, indeed, have widened in recent years. That's because while some countries, most notably the United States, were sharply increasing already high prison populations, others were holding them stable—or even reducing them. In Germany, where the official response to crime for more than 120 years has been mainly "non-custodial," as one study (Oberwittler and Hofer 2005) puts it, the rate of imprisonment fell during the 1980s, while that in the United States skyrocketed. (The German rate rose somewhat in the 1990s, but at last count was still just about one ninth the U.S. rate; Oberwittler and Hofer 2005). Similarly, despite some rises in serious crime, the prison population in Switzerland was lower in 2002 than it had been 20 years before (and less than one tenth the U.S. rate; Eisner and Killias 2004).

There are some exceptions to this relatively soft trajectory in most of the advanced industrial countries. In the Netherlands, a country with a long tradition of using prisons very sparingly, prison populations have rapidly increased since the early 1990s, at a pace much faster than that of any other European country (Downes and van Swaaningen 2007). In the United Kingdom, a relatively high rate of imprisonment (by European standards) has increased substantially since the 1990s to become Western Europe's highest. And in both countries, a new language of punitiveness has partly replaced what was historically an ethos of tolerance in the treatment of offenders. But it's important to keep these changes in perspective. Sharp increases in the Dutch prison population have left that country with an incarceration rate that remains only about one sixth that of the United States and only one fifth that of Russia.

Why does a more punitive approach to crime so often predict higher levels of violence? Partly, as I've said, because excessive punishment can itself become a cause of crime—an issue we'll take up again in a moment. But also in part because harsh punishment tends to go along with and exacerbate a whole package of other social attitudes and policies that join to breed high levels of violence. The societies that punish offenders harshly are also harsh in other ways—tolerating great inequalities of income and life conditions (and usually of race and gender), offering few supports for families and children, and often subjecting many of their people to systematic neglect and even violence on the part of authorities.

C. DIVERSITY

A more benign explanation, which is often applied especially to the United States, holds that we have unusually high rates of violent crime because of our unusual ethnic and racial diversity. This is not the racist viewpoint I've talked about before, but an argument—often not very clearly thought out—that there is something about pluralism or difference in itself that causes crime. Recently, some version of this argument has been used, both in the United States and other countries, in support of more restrictive immigration policies. Crime—whether in the United States or France or even Greece—is said to be a problem mainly brought into the country by foreigners who don't understand "our" culture or respect "our" institutions.

The kernel of truth in this view is that violent crime is often particularly severe in societies where some racial, ethnic, or national groups are systematically disadvantaged by historical circumstances and social policy. But the key is that they are disadvantaged—not simply that they are different.

Among other things, this argument greatly underestimates how diverse many other advanced industrial societies have become. Americans often think of European countries as being very homogeneous, and there was a time when they were; but that has changed, often dramatically, with the coming of globalization and the massive migration to Europe of people from Africa, the Middle East, and the Caribbean—and almost equally massive migrations within Europe, from the south to the north and from the east to the west. That mass migration of people has transformed most European countries into multicultural societies, often in a very short time. Even in a country like Switzerland, roughly one fifth of the population today is foreign-born (Eisner and Killias 2004). In the United Kingdom, Germany, France, and the Netherlands, the presence of racial and ethnic minorities, especially in the cities, is an inescapable aspect of modern life. Yet despite this new heterogeneity, these societies maintain relatively low levels of violence by the standards of much of the rest of the world.

That's not to say, of course, that all is well for ethnic and racial minorities in these countries, or that there is no connection between race, ethnicity, immigration, and crime within them. In most of these countries the relationship between the new immigrants and the native population has been uneasy and sometimes volatile—as shown most spectacularly in large-scale rioting by urban minority youth in France in recent years, as well as ethnocentric violence directed against immigrant communities. In many European countries, minorities now make up a starkly disproportionate part of the prison population. In Germany, the number of immigrants—including so called *resettlers,* ethnic Germans formerly living in Russia and other countries—in the prison population has "dramatically increased" in recent years (Oberwittler and Hofer 2005). In Switzerland, a stunning two-thirds of prison inmates are now "non-Swiss" (Eisner and Killias 2004). The proportion of foreign prisoners in the penal systems of other European countries ranges from about 15 percent in England and Wales to 18 percent in Denmark; 21 percent in France; 26 percent in Sweden; roughly 33 percent in the Netherlands, Italy, and Spain; and better than 40 percent in Austria and Greece (International Centre for Prison Studies 2007).

The best evidence suggests that this is partly because minorities— especially youth—are more likely to be monitored and tracked by police and other authorities and thus more likely to be channeled into the criminal justice system and, at least in some places, punished more severely when they are. But it is also partly because rates of serious crime are often higher among these immigrant populations—especially among second-generation youth (Janson 2004; Junger-Tas 2004; Oberwittler and Hofer 2005).

This is a very complicated issue, and it depends on exactly what countries the immigrants come from and where they end up—and on the conditions they encounter when they arrive. It's not that immigration, in itself, predictably causes crime—although that is a common complaint in many countries around the world, from the United States to France, the Netherlands, and Germany, and even Russia. Research in many countries and among many different ethnic groups suggests a more complex pattern. Often, when immigrants first arrive in a new country they are *less* likely to commit serious crimes than the native population, not more—a phenomenon that appears, for example, in recent studies of youth violence (Sampson, Morenoff, and Raudenbush 2005) and domestic violence (Frias and Angel 2005). Something happens, however, after some immigrant groups have been in a country for a longer time. They may encounter systematic discrimination and are often confined to the worst jobs and poorest neighborhoods. It's at that point that crime rates—along with other problems, including psychiatric disorders and drug abuse—often rise among the second and third generations.[1]

We'll look more directly at the (strong) connections between social disadvantage and violence in a moment, but for now, it's important to note that although in most countries some minority groups are indeed disproportionately represented in crime (and in the criminal justice system), the growing diversity of those countries has usually not translated into high levels of violent crime, or changed the balance between high-violence and low-violence countries. Serious violence remains low in those countries where it was low before mass immigration, and still far lower than in the high-violence countries, some of which are indeed less

---

[1]One recent study of black Caribbean immigrants to the United States, for example, found that their mental health tended to deteriorate with increasing exposure to American conditions, "which possibly reflects increased societal stress and downward social mobility associated with being Black in America" (Williams, et al. 2007, 52).

diverse. Toronto is one of the most ethnically diverse cities in the world, but maintains a remarkably low rate of violent crime: some Russian cities are far more homogeneous—but far more violent.

D. PROSPERITY

It is sometimes argued that violent crime is a natural outcome of the growth of prosperity or modernity. In this view, crime—even though it fell for many decades before World War II—increased everywhere in the advanced industrial world in the postwar years. As with the argument about diversity, this suggests that violence is an unfortunate byproduct of social trends that we actually want. We want to be pluralistic and tolerant, but the price of that accepting attitude, some people argue, is more crime. Similarly, we want modern freedoms as well as economic progress and the abundance that it brings, but the price of those is more crime (see Wilson, 1992).

The argument often supports a kind of passive pessimism about our ability to reduce the toll of violence. If violent crime is an inevitable accompaniment of growth and affluence, there isn't much we can do about it; obviously, we don't want to reverse course and turn the clock back to a time when everyone was poorer. Crime, accordingly, is something we must "learn to live with."

The biggest problem with this view is fairly obvious, given what we've seen about the distribution of violence around the world in our time: it not only fails to account for the unequal global pattern of violence, but indeed turns reality on its head. It is precisely among the most affluent and modern societies of the world that serious violent crime is usually the lowest. Most people in those societies, whether in Asia, North America, Europe, or the Pacific—with the great exception of the United States—do not have to "learn to live" with violent crime. People in less-developed and less-fortunate parts

TABLE 1 PROSPERITY AND HOMICIDE

population	GDP per capita ($)	Homicide deaths per 100,000
El Salvador	4,900	55.6
Brazil	8,800	23
Russian Federation	12,200	21.6
Mexico	10,700	15.9
Ukraine	7,800	11.7
UNITED STATES	44,000	6.9
Canada	35,600	2.6
Finland	33, 700	2.2
Czech Republic	21,900	1.4
Greece	24,000	1.2
Sweden	32,200	1.2
Switzerland	34,000	1.1
Germany	31,900	0.9
United Kingdom	31,800	0.8
Austria	34,600	0.8
Norway	46,300	0.9
France	31,100	0.7
Japan	35,100	0.6

Source: Homicide rates from World Health Organization, *WHO Report on Violence and Health, 2002.*

of the world, however, often do. As we will see again and again, the stratification of violence goes along with other kinds of social and economic disadvantage.

Table 1 illustrates this connection through the lens of one commonly used measure of prosperity: what economists call *Gross Domestic Product (GDP) per capita*—meaning, roughly, the total wealth of a country divided by its population. Note that with the not unexpected exception of the United States, the countries that score highly on this measure of abundance are the now familiar faces among the least dangerous societies of the world.

With the exception of tiny Luxembourg, at this writing, Norway ranks as the world's wealthiest nation by this measure: it also has one of the world's lowest levels of violent crime. Other very safe countries also cluster at the top of the list: Switzerland, Sweden, Austria, Canada, and Japan. Meanwhile, most of the high-violence societies are at the other end of the scale: Mexico's GDP per capita is less than one fourth of Norway's; Brazil's, about one fifth; El Salvador's, less than one ninth.

What about changes over time? The prosperity argument tells us that rising crime has been an almost inevitable accompaniment of rising abundance since World War II. But although serious violent crime certainly rose in the United States in that period, for other countries the pattern is far more complicated. The kernel of truth in this view is that there probably was a rise—in some places a sharp rise—in property crimes and less-serious forms of violence at various times during the postwar era. Even for these crimes, however, the picture is clouded by the limitations of the conventional crime statistics I've described. Research in several European countries suggests that a substantial part of the apparent rise in crime—at least in the case of violence—had more to do with people's increasing tendency to report it than to an actual increase. Estimates based on data other than police statistics show much less of an increase—if any—in serious crimes of violence in many European countries, in those years (Estrada 2001, 2004; Junger-Tas 2004). A particularly careful study in Sweden, for example, using statistics on people admitted to hospitals for violent injuries, found no significant increase since the 1970s—in contrast to sharp increases reported in police statistics (Estrada 2006).

The evidence on trends in homicide, moreover—the most serious and best-reported of violent crimes—doesn't support the idea that violence has risen across the board along with abundance. In a few European countries, homicide did increase significantly—in percentage terms—from 1960 to the turn of the twenty-first century, but the increases began from such a low starting point that the levels still remain minimal by Third-World (or American) standards. Thus, homicide rose from 0.6 to 1.2 per 100,000 in Sweden and from 0.3 to 0.8 per 100,000 in the Netherlands in those years. In several other advanced countries—including Austria, Finland, France, Germany, Greece, Italy, and Japan—homicide rates fell as abundance increased. Japan's homicide rate in 2002 was less than one third what it was in 1960; in France, the rate was about one half that of 1960. Other rich countries stayed about the same, in terms of the risks of violent death, throughout those four decades (Organization for Economic Cooperation and Development [OECD] 2005).

The pattern is somewhat different for property crimes like theft, auto theft, and burglary. It has often been argued that violent crime and property crime move in different directions in response to growing abundance. As social conditions improve, violence becomes less likely (and less tolerated). At the same time, the greater amount of goods available means that there is more to be stolen, and far more opportunities to steal; and the evidence, although suffering from the weakness of the data on these crimes, tends to support this pattern.

The correlation between relative abundance and relative safety isn't perfect. That's in part because, again, the United States so dramatically throws off the picture at the top—showing in the starkest terms that overall abundance is no guarantee that a society will be secure. More subtly, some of the less-affluent countries in Europe—such as Greece, Portugal, and the Czech Republic—also have low rates of violence, at least as measured by their homicide rates. We will return to ask why these anomalies exist in a moment. But it's clear that, although general prosperity is strongly related to public safety, that's not the whole story. It is possible for a society to be both rich and violent—or to be poor and less so. Some kinds of prosperity "work" in terms of keeping violence low, and the streets and homes relatively safe; others, tragically, do not.

2. EXPLANATIONS THAT WORK

If these common explanations all fall short, are there better ones?

Yes. Although there is much that we don't know about the roots of violent crime, there is also much that we do know. Every society's experience of violence is to some degree unique—rooted in complex historical, cultural, and social developments. But we can see some common forces at work across societies in all corners of the world—societies with very different histories and very different cultures. Understanding those common forces takes us a long way toward unraveling the question of why some societies are more dangerous than others.

It's important to be clear about just what it is we are trying to explain. A phenomenon as complicated as violence involves different levels of explanation. The job of explaining why one society differs from another in the risks of violent crime is different from the job of explaining why, in any given society, one individual becomes involved in violent crime while another does not—why Joe or Ivan picks up a gun, but Bob or Vassili doesn't. Individuals, like societies, have complex and unique histories. We can't necessarily predict how any individual will behave from the wider social conditions that surround them. But those broader conditions are crucial in understanding the overall *risks* of being a perpetrator, or a victim, of violence that any individual faces.

The distinction is important. It's sometimes argued that social conditions cannot explain why people commit crime, because after all, many people experience similar conditions but don't turn to crime. Yet although it's certainly true that people respond to the same social surroundings in different ways, that doesn't tell us that those surroundings are unimportant. Some especially resilient individuals may resist the pressures toward violent crime that exist in the worst slums of Rio de Janeiro or Detroit; but that doesn't mean that the pressures aren't real, or that they are irrelevant in helping us understand why Rio and Detroit are such dangerous places.

Some people feel uneasy, or even indignant, about the very idea that there are social sources of crime, because they think that this is just a way of excusing the behavior of criminals: If we say, for example, that economic inequality tends to breed violent crime, we are sending the message that it's okay if poor people rob or steal. But that doesn't follow. After all, there are criminal justice systems in every society that exist to punish people who break the law, and every society around the world condemns violent crime (or, at least, some of it—an issue to which we'll return). Understanding why some societies are especially likely to produce criminals doesn't let the individual criminal off the hook, but it does provide us with the kind of understanding of the possible causes of individuals' violent behavior without which we cannot hope to develop intelligent policies to prevent it. Imperfect as that understanding may be, it is an essential first step in being able to reduce the intolerable levels of violence suffered by people around the globe.

When we turn to those explanations that meet the test of evidence, we see that there is not just *one* that helps us to understand the roots of violence, but many. Some of them involve broad, structural social and economic conditions. Some involve cultural attitudes—including attitudes about gender relations, the rearing of children, and the

ities of societies to support their most vulnerable members. Some involve particular social policies—regarding the regulation of firearms, for example, or the punishment of offenders. It's important to understand, however, that these are not really separable. They are not a collection of isolated factors or variables—although too often, researchers tend to treat them as if they were. Studies are often designed to tell us, for example, whether it is inequality *or* poverty *or* disrupted families that is responsible for violent crime. But in the real world, all of these problems are deeply intertwined, and tend to reinforce one another. They are parts of a larger whole.

Let's turn now to look at several of the most important of those parts. I won't simply list all of the factors that have been linked by researchers to violent crime: instead, I'll focus on a few that are especially important and that are best supported by the evidence. They include

- Inequality
- Marginal work
- Weak social supports
- Strained families
- Harsh and ineffective criminal justice systems
- Easy access to firearms

I'll look at what we know about the role of each of these in violent crime, and then consider, in the conclusion, what this understanding implies for the future of violence in global society.

A. INEQUALITY

Brazil is one of the most violent counties in the world. It is also one in which the gap between affluent and poor—between "haves" and "have-nots"—is among the most extreme. And within Brazil, the differences in the risks of violence are extreme. In the city of Sao Paulo, the chance of becoming the victim of homicide is almost one hundred times greater in one of the poorest districts than in one of the most affluent (CDC, 2004).

Brazil is an extreme case, but the link between inequality and violent crime is consistently borne out in many different kinds of studies, both within societies and between them. We may, of course, believe whatever we like about the virtues, philosophically or morally, of economic and social equality: but it is hard to dispute that violent crime, as two researchers put it in a classic study (Blau and Blau 1982), is one of the predictable "costs" of inequality, and especially of very wide disparities in social and economic conditions.

That connection helps explain why a country like the United States, which is otherwise so wealthy, can have such high levels of violence; the American variety of abundance goes hand-in-hand with unusually wide disparities between affluent and poor, disparities on a level that isn't seen anywhere else in the advanced industrial world. By the same token, it helps us understand why some countries in the developing world have the highest rates of violence of all.

These relationships, although strong, aren't necessarily simple or easy to define. Inequality can have many different meanings and can be measured in many different ways. When we speak of the effect of inequality on violent crime, we're not talking just about economic inequality in the narrow sense that some people have more income or wealth than others—although that is an important part of the problem. The kind of inequality that seems most associated with violent crime around the world is best understood as a broader and more multifaceted condition of social disadvantage—or what some people have called *social exclusion*. It is a condition that affects virtually every aspect of life—from access to material goods to the quality of family life, to the availability of medical care and other social services, opportunities for political participation, and much more.

To understand these connections, let's first take a look at what some basic figures tell us about inequality and violence around the world today.

To do that, we must first be clear on what we *mean* by economic inequality. One of the ways in which economists often assess inequality within a country is through a measure called the *Gini index*, a mathematical expression of the degree to which household income departs from perfect equality. Thus, if all of the households in a given country had the same income, the Gini index would be zero. A score of one hundred would be at the other end—a perfectly unequal society. The higher a country scores on the Gini index, in short, the greater its degree of economic inequality. Table 2 shows how some countries stack up, in the most current year available, when seen through this lens. We'll include the national homicide death rate as a reminder.

TABLE 2   INEQUALITY AND HOMICIDE

	Gini Index	Homicide death rate per 100,000
Brazil	56.7	23.0
Mexico	54.6	15.9
Colombia	53.8	61.6
El Salvador	52.5	55.6
UNITED STATES	45.0	6.9
Russia	40.5	21.6
United Kingdom	36.8	0.8
Canada	33.1	2.6
Norway	25.8	0.9
Sweden	25.0	1.2
Denmark	23.2	1.1

Source: Gini figures from *World Factbook*, 2007; Homicide rates from World Health Organization, *World Report on Violence and Health*, 2002.

At the bottom, or more equal, end of the scale are a number of Western European countries we have encountered already—Denmark at the very lowest point, then Sweden and Norway, all with a Gini index of around 25 or less. A bit higher up is Canada, and the United Kingdom is a bit higher still. Russia—perhaps not surprisingly—comes in at more than 40. The United States—not for the first time—is startlingly out of line on this scale: With a Gini index of about 45, it is, by this measure, roughly twice as unequal as Denmark, and it looms above all of the advanced industrial societies on this table (and for that matter, all the others not on this table).

Yet the United States, although highly unusual among the advanced nations, doesn't by any means top the list of countries on this table with the most extreme inequality. That distinction goes to several countries in Latin America—El Salvador, Colombia, Mexico, and at the very top, Brazil.

Table 2 doesn't show it, but in many countries—including the United States—the Gini index has risen rapidly in recent years, a trend with obviously troubling implications for violent crime. For now, however, look at the raw figures on homicide deaths up against the Gini index. The figures follow each other with startling predictability. The Latin American societies with some of the world's worst levels of violence are also among the most starkly unequal; the affluent Western European societies have the least inequality and among the lowest levels of violent crime; and the United States stands alone among the advanced industrial societies as by far both the most violent and the most economically divided.

We can look at inequality in other ways and still come up with a similar picture. One way to measure economic disparities is to compare how much income the best off people enjoy with that of the worst off—

the top versus the bottom. Obviously, if a handful of people rake in a disproportionate share of the country's income while those on the bottom of the social ladder get very little, the society can be considered very unequal. And once again, the global pattern we saw for the Gini index—and the connection with violence—jumps out clearly from the bare figures.

In Sweden and Norway, the top 10 percent of households bring in a little more than five times as much income as the bottom 10 percent does. That is far from an equal share, but in other countries the disparities are much greater. In Canada, the top 10 percent brings in about $8^1/_2$ times what the bottom 10 percent does. In the United States, the share of the top 10 percent is a startling 17 times that of the bottom 10 percent; in Russia, it is 23; in Brazil, it is about 45; and in El Salvador—not coincidentally, one of the most dangerous places in the world—it is 58. (These figures are somewhat dated, but it is likely, for reasons we will consider later, that these gaps are even wider today in the United States and Latin America.)

The wide gap in some countries between rich and poor reflects both an especially large share at the top and an especially small one at the bottom. Thus, in Sweden the top 10 percent takes in about 20 percent of the total income. That's still a disproportionate share, to be sure, but it pales beside the situation in the United States, where the top 10 percent takes more than 30 percent of the total income, or in Russia or El Salvador, where the figure is closer to 39 percent—that is, one tenth of the population takes in almost two fifths of the total income. Similar wide disparities appear at the lower end of the scale. In Norway and Sweden, the bottom tenth of the population takes in around 4 percent of the total income; in the United States and Russia, less than 2 percent; and in Brazil and El Salvador, considerably less than 1 percent.

What we see in rough outline by looking at these bare figures has been confirmed again and again in more elaborate studies that use complex statistical techniques to sort out the specific effects of inequality—often measured by the Gini index—on violent crime (see, e.g., Chamlin and Cochran 2006; Pratt and Godsey 2003). These studies, conducted both internationally and within specific countries, states, and cities, provide a convincing array of evidence linking economic inequality to crime (for a recent review, see Pratt and Cullen 2005; for an earlier discussion, see Currie 1985, Chapter 5). The better the data used to measure violent crime, the clearer these connections appear: and they are stronger for more serious kinds of violence. Thus, studies that link economic inequality to medical data on homicide deaths have turned up a very strong connection between the two for many years (for recent examples, see Butchart and Engstrom 2002; Pickett, Mookherjee, and Wilkinson, 2005). The connection shows up less strongly in studies using police report figures on nonfatal crimes—probably in part because of the limitations of the data, partly because homicide may be more closely linked to extremes of inequality. Studies based on victim surveys, despite their tendency to understate levels of violence in highly unequal countries, still routinely affirm the links between inequality and violence. The study mentioned previously of victimization data in 27 countries, for example, shows a strong connection between the Gini index and levels of assault and robbery (Van Wilsem 2004; see also Nilsson and Estrada 2006).

Being at the bottom of the economic ladder, even in wealthy countries, means being poorer—at least, as compared with others in your society. Thus, it's not surprising that many studies have also found violent crime to be specifically related to poverty as well as to inequality (Pratt and Cullen 2005; Currie 1985, 1998). The connection holds true for different states or local areas in the United States and other countries:

poorer people and poorer places within countries tend to suffer the worst violence—along with a host of other troubles.

But the link between violence and poverty is a complicated one. There are poor countries with relatively low levels of violent crime, and in Europe, some countries that are only modestly affluent—like Greece, the Czech Republic, or Slovenia—have a relatively low level of violence, at least as measured by their rates of violent death. This suggests that it isn't simply the fact of not having much income that is most important in explaining violence: some kinds of poverty may be more consequential than others.

Like inequality, poverty can mean many different things, and can be measured in many different ways. Some scholars, for example, make a distinction between *absolute* and *relative* poverty. *Absolute poverty* means not having enough money to meet some defined standard of what it takes to buy the basic necessities of life—food, shelter, clothing, and so on. This is how we officially measure poverty in the United States. The federal government establishes a so-called poverty line (approximately $20,000 a year for a family of four in 2006), and defines people who have an income less than that as poor. *Relative poverty,* in contrast, is not a measure of whether you have enough money to obtain the basics of life, but whether your income allows you to have a standard of living that is at least reasonably close to what others around you enjoy. There are several ways to measure relative poverty, but the basic idea is to define as poor those people who make less than a certain proportion of the average income in their society. It is a measure, in short, of distance from the middle—of how far families or individuals are from the common standard of living of others in their society. And it turns out that societies in which larger numbers of people are relatively deprived in this sense are often the ones with the worst levels of violent crime–which may help us explain how a wealthy society can be riven by violence while others that are less wealthy are not.

Let's take a look at how some countries stand on a measure of relative poverty—defined here as having less than 40 percent of the country's median household income. We'll look specifically at the rates for children under 18, because it makes sense to think that growing up in a condition of economic exclusion as a child may be especially destructive to personality and opportunity in ways that increase the risks of violence.

By this measure, in Russia and Mexico, about 17 percent of children live in families that are relatively poor. At the other end of the scale, the proportion of children in relative poverty is only 2.6 percent in France, 1.8 percent in Sweden, 1.6 percent in Norway, and 1.5 percent in Denmark. It's only a little over 3 percent in the Czech Republic and Slovenia. The proportion is a startling 14 percent in the United States—meaning that, as with the Gini index of inequality, by this measure of poverty, the United States resembles Russia or Mexico much more than it does Sweden or France.

In the United States, about one child in seven is relatively poor; in Norway, one child in sixty-three. Some of the advanced countries in Western Europe have, for all practical purposes, eliminated relative poverty in this sense among children under 18. Closer to home, Canada has relative child poverty rates that are only a bit more than half those in the United States.

Note that some of the less-affluent countries in Europe—the Czech Republic, for example—have very low levels of relative poverty. Although the country isn't as affluent as its neighbors in Western Europe, or the United States, the proportion of people with substantially less than the average is low—dramatically so by comparison to the United States, as is the homicide rate.

In many countries—including some that used to be relatively egalitarian, like the United Kingdom and the Netherlands, as well as some that weren't, like Russia—relative poverty has increased, often sharply, in recent years. As we'll see in more detail later, these are often countries where the number of people behind bars is growing as well. Why that should be so—why we are seeing in many countries a sort of pulling away of the top from the bottom, and what that means for the future of violent crime and the systems of criminal justice—is an issue to which we will return. For now, suffice it to say that like the phenomenon of inequality to which it is closely related, the fact of being relatively poorer by comparison to one's fellow citizens is directly linked to the experience of violent crime.

How do we explain why economic inequality breeds violent crime? The best evidence is that it does so in several ways at once.

, Particularly in the developing world, high levels of inequality go together with absolute poverty—deep material deprivation—among people at the bottom end of the social and economic ladder. In some countries in Latin America, Africa, or the Caribbean, for example, large numbers of people simply do not have enough legitimate income to live on, and may need to supplement their legitimate resources with illegitimate ones in order to survive at a minimal level.

In more developed societies, where the overall level of economic well-being is higher, the more important effect of inequality lies in its impact on less tangible things, such as social cohesion, values, attitudes, people's sense of being bonded to society and their willingness to accept its rules. Some criminologists argue that extremes of inequality in modern capitalist societies create a *strain* between peoples' desires for material possessions and status on the one hand and their realistically limited abilities to achieve those desires in legitimate ways on the other (Merton 1957). Where a culture holds out owning expensive things and having an affluent lifestyle as the most important sources of self-esteem and even of identity, those who are unable—because of poor skills or inadequate education or discrimination—to fulfill those wants in legitimate ways may respond by rejecting the rules that keep them from engaging in illicit behavior, including violence (or drug dealing, which is closely associated with violence). The American sociologist Robert K. Merton first developed this theory in the 1930s; but it may be even more relevant today, at a time when the level of wealth at the top in the United States (and many other societies) is considerably greater, the contrast with poverty more glaring, and the impact of a pervasive consumer culture much more powerful (Currie 1997).

Arguably as important, however, is the effect of inequality on other key institutions: what it does to the stability of families, to the capacity of parents to care for and supervise children, and to the cohesion of the communities in which people live. Inequality and poverty are not merely economic conditions. Particularly in the most disadvantaged communities, whether in highly developed societies or in Third World countries, inequality and poverty of economic resources tend to go along with a whole host of adverse conditions that powerfully affect the risks that someone will either engage in violence or be a victim of it. That includes importantly, the absence of supportive services from governments, such as childcare, health care, and mental health services, a problem we'll take up in a moment. It also includes more subtle kinds of deprivation and social exclusion: a lack of meaningful things to do with one's time, inadequate and alienating schools, the lack of stable role models for the young, and the absence of channels for political participation or influence over the conditions that affect one's life (Pantazis, Gordon, and Levitas 2006).

These extremely disadvantaged communities may also provide built-in negative influences that also raise the risks of violence. One is the availability of what some criminologists call *illegitimate opportunities*—opportunities to become involved in dangerous and illegal activities. In some communities around the world, there are violent gangs or drug-dealing organizations for young people to join just outside their front doors; in others, nothing of the kind exists. And where a community is already suffused with violence, there is a strong incentive for youth to take up weapons for protection or for status, which can lead to a destructive cycle of preemptive violence, retaliation, and further violence. These threats in turn may result in more young people being arrested, sentenced, and sent to prison, rendering them much less able to escape the confines of poverty and marginality in the future. Harsh inequality, in short, sets in motion a set of processes that are self-sustaining and mutually supportive.

Many studies suggest that the combination of economic inequality with *racial* inequality is especially destructive (Blau and Blau 1982; Currie 1985; Land, McCall, and Cohen 1990). We can see this connection clearly in the United States, where a long history of racial inequality and injustice within a generally affluent society has contributed mightily to the country's unusually severe problem of violent crime.

The raw figures on the risks of violent death among the races speak eloquently and painfully to the effects of that history. In the United States as a whole, the homicide death rate for young black men is roughly four times the overall youth rate, which, as we've seen, towers above that of any other advanced industrial society. It is more than ten times the rate for what our Census Bureau calls "non-Hispanic whites," which is itself far higher than the rate for youth of all races in almost every other advanced industrial society. The homicide rate for black *women* in this age group is double that of white *men*, upending the usual relationships between gender and violence.

In California, homicide accounts for nearly three out of five of all deaths suffered by black men ages 15 to 29, versus 8 percent for white, non-Hispanic men that age.

In many states with large urban black ghettos, these numbers rise even higher, to levels that are found nowhere else outside of the most violence-ridden countries of the Third World, as Chart 3 illustrates. Young black men in Louisiana have homicide death rates that are exceeded only by youth in Colombia, and are actually higher than those of young men in El Salvador; black youth in Michigan (and some other states) aren't far behind. When it comes to violence, they are simply in a different world than their counterparts in countries like France, the United Kingdom, Japan, or Canada. Again, a look at Chart 3 (based on data for various years around the turn of the 21st century) shows that

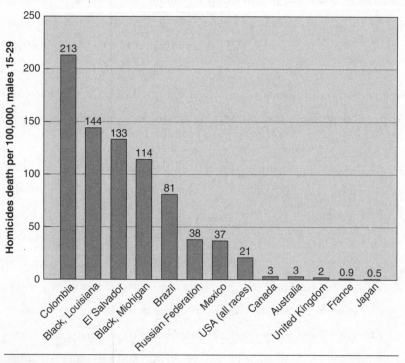

CHART 3   YOUNG MEN AND HOMICIDE
Source: Data from Krug et al (2000) and CDC figures.

overall rate for youth in the United States—including whites—is far higher than that of young men in the other advanced industrial societies, so race is only part of the picture: but it is a very important part. (A similar picture generally holds for nonfatal violence, including domestic violence; black Americans face higher risks across the board.)

How do we explain the special vulnerability of black Americans to violence? Research makes it clear that it's primarily because a historical legacy of discrimination has kept blacks disproportionately subject to the kinds of social and economic disadvantages that tend to breed violence among people of *any* race or ethnicity (Brown, et al. 2003). Studies show repeatedly that when the effects of such ills as social exclusion, mass unemployment, family disruption, and poverty are taken into account, the higher rates of both street and domestic violence among blacks are largely explained (see, e.g., Benson, et al. 2004; Field and Caetano 2004; Krivo and Peterson 1994; Sampson, Morenoff, and Raudenbush 2005). In the United States, as in some other countries, blacks are much more likely to suffer from the most extreme levels of economic deprivation, and, importantly, to live in areas of *concentrated* poverty—neighborhoods where a very substantial proportion of the population is poor. They are also, as we'll see, more likely to suffer from extreme levels of joblessness. And the research probably understates the significance of that legacy, because some of its effects are hard to capture with the relatively blunt tools of social science. It's hard to measure, for example, the corrosive effects of long-term denial of opportunities on such things as community stability, hope for the future, and the sense of self-worth, but all of these may have an important role in preventing violence. Some studies, too, argue that the special unfairness of racial discrimination creates a sting all its own—breeding a degree of anger, alienation, and disaffiliation that goes beyond the effects of economic inequality alone (Blau and Blau 1982).

(There is a similar, although not as great, disparity for Hispanics in the United States. Not only are young Hispanic men disproportionately likely to die by violence in the United States, but young women of Hispanic origin are as well. Violence is the second leading cause of death among Hispanic youth in America. Hispanic youth in the United States are as likely to die by violence as Hispanic youth in Mexico. Violence is the third leading cause of death for Asian Americans and the fourth leading cause of death for non-Hispanic whites.)

The strong links between racial inequality and violent crime don't appear only in the United States; we see them in stark relief in South Africa, for example, where—although the data are not very reliable—it's generally agreed that the level of serious violent crime is among the highest in the world. In Brazil, too, blacks face higher risks of violence. Even in the low-crime countries of Western Europe, racial and ethnic minorities turn up disproportionately in the statistics on violent crime—and, accordingly, in the statistics on who is in prison. Afro-Caribbeans in England, Muslims in France and Germany, and Finns and Turks in Sweden are all overrepresented in the statistics on crime and incarceration. In all of these societies, as is true for the United States, minority status influences crime because it is so closely connected with other aspects of social and economic exclusion—long-term poverty, poor employment, school failure, and segregated communities.

Race is only one of the inequalities that can exacerbate violence; gender is another.

Societies in which women are routinely denied the economic opportunities that men enjoy put women at greater risk of being victims of violence in several ways. They make it harder for women to escape from abusive relationships, which may indeed be considered normal in those societies, or to find enough support to live independently when they do escape (we will explore these issues in more detail in a moment). Restricted opportunities and unequal pay also promote what is often called the *feminization of poverty*, meaning that women are far more likely than men to be poor, especially if they are not married, and thus suffer the multiple risks that accompany poverty. In particular, women who are single parents face not only greater chances of being poor, but also greater risks of victimization by violence over and above those that stem from poverty alone (see Nilsson and Estrada 2006; Pantazis, et al. 2006). That is partly because they suffer greater social isolation and are more vulnerable to crime as a result—as are their children.

When we speak of social disadvantage, in other words, we are speaking disproportionately about *women's* social disadvantage, because a disproportionate number of those people in the most deprived conditions are women, both in the most advanced industrial societies and in the developing world. But like economic inequality generally, the disparities are greater and more consequential in some societies than others. In a number of Third World countries, most women—especially low-income women—are extremely dependent on men for support and often for basic survival. In most of the advanced countries, women enjoy both formal legal equality and a much wider range of economic and educational opportunities. Even in those societies, women bear a disproportionate share of the burden of social exclusion. But the differences between these settings are great, and they go a long way toward explaining why women are much more likely to suffer violence in some countries than in others.

Inequality and poverty are profoundly shaped by the possibilities for meaningful and sustaining work and the availability of public supports and social services—issues to which we will now turn.

B. MARGINAL WORK

All over the world—whether in Detroit, Glasgow, Paris, Moscow, Sao Paulo, or Johannesburg—it is young men without good jobs or prospects who are usually most involved in violence, both as victims and perpetrators. This is not a new phenomenon; since the nineteenth century, if not before, scholars have understood that there is a strong connection between work—or the lack of it—and crime.

The connection is complicated, because work (and unemployment) can mean many different things, all of which have different relevance to the problem of violent crime. The evidence suggests that it is not just having some kind of job, or not having one, that is most important when it comes to crime, but whether the job that you are in—or hope to be able to get in the future—is the kind that allows you to make a decent living, as your society defines it; fosters a sense of purpose and self-esteem; and promises a secure future as a respected member of your community: what I will call *inclusive work*. Having such a job is, of course, no guarantee against crime; after all, some people with excellent jobs—heads of corporations, high-level government officials—commit very serious crimes with staggering social costs (see, e.g., Rosoff, Pontell, and Tillman 2007). But not having this kind of work, or the expectation of it, especially when you are young, is a central part of the larger condition of social exclusion that raises the risks dramatically of being involved in violence. Societies where a substantial and concentrated population, especially the young, are stuck over the long term in what I will call *marginal work*—meaning not only not working at all, or working only intermittently, but also working only in very low-paying and often demeaning jobs—are likely to be societies that suffer a great deal of violent crime.

Why is marginal work so predictably connected to high levels of violent crime? As with the links between inequality and crime, there are many reasons, and they are not mutually exclusive: they reinforce each other.

First, because work is what most strongly determines income and economic status, marginal work is a prime contributor to poverty and social exclusion. (This is especially true in those countries—including the United States and many less developed countries—where there are only minimal public income supports to buffer the absence of income from work.) The scarcity of inclusive work makes *illegal* work—like dealing drugs or guns, or engaging in prostitution—highly attractive, even if it is dangerous and not, over the long run, especially rewarding. In a more subtle way, work also provides a life structure that helps keep people from involvement in violent crime. People who are at work are not out on the street corner or in the bar; they are behind the store counter, on the shop floor, in the office. This means they are not only less likely to be pulled into committing violence, but also less likely to be a victim.

In less tangible (but very real) ways, inclusive work has a variety of mutually reinforcing social and psychological effects that diminish the appeal of violence. In most cultures, it is one of the main sources of self-respect and the esteem of others; indeed, the work we do or do not do is a key aspect of our very definition of who we are and what our place in our society is. Being out of real work for an extended period of time is likely to breed a sense of failure and a loss of self-respect, which in turn makes the search for *alternative* sources of respect, including illegal ones, more likely (Bourgois, 2002). It is sometimes argued, in fact, that much violent crime is ultimately about respect, which helps explain its frequently "senseless" character. Often, violent crime is not instrumental in the narrow sense (although sometimes it is); it is an assertion, sometimes a desperate one, of self, and a demand for respect and recognition. You shoot someone because they looked at you in the wrong way. You go home to get your semi-automatic pistol because someone "disrespected" you in the street or the basketball court. Obviously, the lack of meaningful work isn't the entire explanation for this kind of response, but the absence of a sense of approval and inclusion, of being a respected and self-respecting member of the productive community, is often a key part of it. Inclusive work is important, in other words, for more than economic reasons: our place (or our lack of one) in the world of productive work cuts to some of the most fundamental emotional needs we have as members of a society.

Inclusive work is also a necessary prerequisite to other life conditions that inhibit getting involved in crime. A good job makes it possible to define yourself as the head of a family, as someone with responsibilities, someone who can support others. Research on the life course of people who break the law when they're young, for example, shows that getting a steady job is one of the most important turning points that help to keep them from crime as they get older (Sampson and Laub 1993).

Beyond its effects on individuals, joblessness also has destructive impacts on whole communities. Communities where large numbers of people are routinely out of work may, over time, breed a culture in which legitimate work is seen as unattainable or even undesirable. Communities where large numbers of adults are out of work are also communities that lack positive role models and mentors for young people growing up, as well as social networks and connections to the legitimate working world (Sullivan 1989), which makes it that much harder for young people, even with the motivation, to land the kind of work that could include them securely in the larger society. They are communities, in short, that lack the capacity to provide the young with the expectation of a rewarding future and to inspire them with a reasonable confidence that if they work hard and stay out of trouble, they will achieve a respected place in their society.

Marginal work also contributes to violent crime through its destructive impact on families. We will look more at the role of the family in violent crime shortly, but for now, suffice it to say that marginal work is deeply implicated in both violence against women in the home and in child abuse and neglect. Being stuck in marginal work, for example, makes men more inclined to abuse their partners; simultaneously, the lack of opportunities for good work helps keep women trapped in abusive relationships (Websdale and Johnson 1997). In addition, the long hours often required to make a living when the only work available pays poorly make it difficult for working parents to nurture and supervise their children.

For all these reasons, studies suggest that drawing more people into inclusive work can bring down the rate of violent crime significantly. In the United States, the long economic boom that took place during the 1990s brought great numbers of young people, many of whom had never worked before, into legitimate jobs; not coincidentally, the same years also saw one of the sharpest drops in violent crime in American history.

Understanding the connection between marginal work and violence helps explain why the United States, which is often said to be a country that enjoys very low unemployment and an exemplary record of creating jobs, nevertheless stands out as the most violent of advanced societies. The United States is often compared favorably in this respect to Europe in particular, where, according to the conventional wisdom, the problem of unemployment is far worse. At first glance, then, it might seem that the example of the United States —a country with low unemployment but unusually high violence—casts doubt on the link between work and crime: but that would be mistaken. First, even if we rely on the conventional (and, as we'll see, highly inadequate) measures of unemployment, the idea that U.S. has performed much better than other advanced industrial countries is misleading. Within Europe, there are indeed countries—including France and Germany—where rates of unemployment are higher than those in the United States, but there are also others, including Sweden, Norway, the Netherlands, Austria, and Switzerland (and in Asia, Japan) where unemployment rates are lower, and have been, in many cases, for decades. Beyond that, however, the way in which unemployment is usually measured minimizes the seriousness of the job problem in the United States, in several ways.

First—a problem we've seen before in looking at the limits of crime statistics—our unemployment figures are skewed by the fact that great numbers of unemployed or marginally employed people are either behind bars or homeless—and in either case, they are not counted in the unemployment statistics, which, like the victimization data, are derived from household surveys. As a result, a substantial proportion of the people most disconnected from inclusive work fall off the statistical radar screen. With more than two million prisoners behind bars on any given day in America—many of whom were marginally employed before they went to prison—and another several hundred thousand homeless, the impact this has in artificially reducing the jobless figures is quite significant. Adding, say, two million people to the official count of the unemployed (just over seven million, on average, in 2007) raises the unemployment rate in that year by well over one fourth, thus pushing us past several other advanced industrial nations (cf. Western, Pettit, and Guetzkow 2002). To be fair, of course, we must also do the same addition for other countries; but doing so would not change their unemployment rates to the same degree, because the proportion of their population who are incarcerated or homeless is nowhere near as great.

Even more important, the conventional definition of *unemployment* excludes many of the people I am calling *marginally employed,* and so it gives a sharply limited picture of the extent of the job problem.

In the United States, the government defines *unemployment* not, as one might expect, as the condition of not having a job, but as two conditions: not having a job, and not having *looked* for a job in the past month. But this means that many people who don't have jobs are not counted as unemployed; indeed, it means that many of the people who are arguably the *most* marginal are left out of the count. People who don't have a job but have not looked for one recently are either called *discouraged workers* or *out of the labor force,* depending on why they haven't sought work. (Among other things, this means that studies that try to link crime with joblessness by relying on the official unemployment rate will understate the connection, because they will miss this large category of people, many of whom are thoroughly disengaged from the world of work.) Adding those who aren't looking for work to those who are officially unemployed produces much higher numbers of people who are jobless (roughly doubling the official unemployment rate, according to some estimates).

The conventional statistics on unemployment also do not include people who do have jobs but are working only part-time when they need a full-time job, or who are stuck in work that pays very poorly, is unstable, and doesn't offer opportunities for moving up to something better, and thus contributes to social and economic exclusion: and the United States has an unusually high proportion of people who fit that description. The wages that American workers receive in lower-level jobs are only a fraction of those received by many of their counterparts in Europe. The result is that the problem of what some call *working poverty* is far more prevalent in the United States than it is in most other advanced industrial societies, where having a job is much more likely to mean having a living wage—and in all probability having an array of guaranteed social benefits to go with it. In the United States, there are several million people who work full-time and yet are unable to make enough to rise above the official poverty level. They are not counted among the unemployed, but they are certainly not fortunate enough to have the kind of work that can reliably promote social inclusion. The distinction is important, because social policies in many countries, particularly the United States and the United Kingdom, have been heavily oriented toward coercing people into any kind of work, no matter how poorly paying or "dead-end" the job may be. That may help boost the employment figures, but whether it can do much to reduce violent crime is another question altogether.

Looking solely at the official unemployment rate also obscures the fact that the social conditions of people who are jobless in the United States (as in the developing world) tend to be worse—often strikingly worse—than those of their counterparts in other advanced industrial societies. We'll look at this issue more closely shortly, but for now it's enough to point out that the United States is distinctive among affluent societies in the skimpiness of the income supports it provides for people who are out of work. Overall income supports for families are considerably higher, and benefits paid specifically to the unemployed far more generous, in most other advanced industrial countries. The result is that to be jobless in America is typically a different experience, with different consequences, than it is in many of those countries—harsher, more insecure, and more destructive in its impact on individuals, families, and communities.

Finally, and crucially important, focusing on the overall *national* unemployment rate, masks the fact that, like violence, marginal work is unevenly distributed in America (and other countries). It is far more common, and more severe, in some places and among some groups than others. So although the national unemployment rate may seem relatively low, unemployment is startlingly high in many inner cities—

especially among minority men—even measured in the conventional (and misleading) way; and it is far higher when we count those who are "out of the labor force." In some of the most violence-ridden urban ghettos in the United States, the proportion of young men without any job is stratospheric. Indeed, in many of those communities, only a small minority of young people work in legitimate jobs. These are, unsurprisingly, the same neighborhoods where the number of people sent to prison is astonishingly high.

In short, the problem of marginal work and the resulting social exclusion is far more pervasive in the United States than many realize, and it is closely linked to the country's unusually high rates of violence. Conditions in some countries in the developing world are even worse. In many cities in Latin America and Africa, the proportion of low-income youth who are working in a legitimate job is tiny. Even in places where the economy has enjoyed significant growth overall, it has too often been what some economists call *jobless growth,* and has flooded the cities with massive numbers of people without any realistic expectation of inclusive work (Ayres 1998). Similarly, the destruction of traditional sources of work and livelihood in the course of a rapid transition to a market economy has been dramatic in Russia and much of Eastern Europe (Karstedt 2003), and in China as well (Liu and Messner 2004), where wrenching economic change has created a large and volatile "floating" population of the uprooted and minimally employed.

This is not to idealize the situation in other developed countries. In all of them, the problem of assuring steady and meaningful work, especially for youth, is one of the toughest they face, and some have done a much better job of addressing it than others. One way to measure this is by looking at the proportion of young people ages fifteen to nineteen who are not in school, at work, or in training of any kind. In this respect, the developed countries present an extraordinarily varied picture: The proportion of youth who are cut off from productive activity in this sense is very low in such countries as Norway, Denmark, Sweden, the Netherlands, and Germany; relatively high in the United States (even without factoring in the ways in which the conventional statistics understate youth joblessness in America); still higher in the United Kingdom; and even higher in France (UNICEF 2007, 21). In the slums of Glasgow, the *banlieues* of Paris, or the bleak housing estates of Liverpool, there are heavy concentrations of young men with no real job and no expectation of one in the future, and large numbers of parents who are either jobless or trapped in low-paying work. Obviously, that doesn't bode well for the future. Even in some of the traditionally most inclusive countries of Western Europe, the failure to find ways to put the young on a path to constructive work could undo their success in reducing violent crime.

C. WEAK SOCIAL SUPPORTS

Economic inequality and marginal work, then, are two closely related aspects of the larger condition of social exclusion that often join together to breed violent crime. Another is the absence of strong supports—whether provided by government or other institutions—to promote peoples' well-being and protect against economic deprivation and insecurity. Societies that make a strong commitment to providing those supports are less likely to suffer high rates of violent crime than those that do not (Cullen 1994). We know this from a variety of sources of evidence. Countries that spend a higher proportion of their wealth on social services, especially for children and families, tend to have lower levels of serious violent crime (Messner and Rosenfeld 2001; Pampel and Gartner 1995; Pratt and Cullen 2005; Pratt and Godsey 2003). The same pattern shows up within individual countries: providing poor families with higher welfare support, for example, helps diminish the rate of some kinds of crime (DeFronzo, 1997).

There are several reasons why this connection should prevail. For one thing, strong social supports are one of the most important ways in which the potentially destructive effects of joblessness or severe economic deprivation are buffered. These benefits mean that people facing difficult times in their lives because of low income or losing a job or poor health are not thereby condemned to desperate conditions. Social spending on job creation and training can help give vulnerable people the skills they need to participate in the world of inclusive work, countering the kind of marginality that, as we saw, so often breeds violence. Investment in high-quality health care for everyone can lower the risks of violence in many ways as well, by providing prenatal care to ensure that children are born healthy, enabling people with mental health problems to get the attention they need, and providing effective medical intervention for victims of violence.

In a more subtle sense, the degree to which a society provides for its citizens in these ways profoundly influences important social and cultural attitudes and values—especially the sense of social solidarity or social cohesion. It affects whether people are able to feel a part of their society— to feel that they are being treated well and that they will be taken care of. Generous and inclusive public benefits help build that sense of connection; the failure of government or other social agencies to provide them can lead to alienation, antagonism, and resentment.

Societies differ greatly in their commitment to providing these supports for their citizens. On the simplest level, the amount of GDP spent on public social benefits—what economists call *transfers*—varies widely among different countries (even within the affluent, developed world); and outside the developed world, the variation is even greater.

At the start of the twenty-first century, for example, that proportion ranged from about 29 percent in countries like Sweden, Denmark, and France to only about 14 percent in the United States and less than 10 percent in Mexico. The United States' level of spending on social services, in other words, was less than half that of some European industrial societies—and actually closer to that of some poorer countries like Turkey (UNICEF 2005).

This is the same pattern we saw for measures of poverty and income inequality: the countries with wide inequality and much poverty tend also to be those that spend relatively little to support their vulnerable citizens, instead leaving economic and social well-being up to the efforts of individuals and families—particularly on their success, or lack of it, in the labor market. In those societies, people who do not fare well in the world of work wind up falling to the bottom—and the bottom is typically very far down.

It isn't surprising that poverty and extremes of inequality go together with low levels of public spending, because one of the main purposes of that spending is to reduce them, and some advanced societies have been remarkably successful in doing so. No country has eliminated poverty altogether—but some have come fairly close. One way to measure this effect is to look at the difference between the poverty rate a country *would* have were it not for government efforts to reduce it, versus the rate it actually has after government spending. Once again, the differences, even among rich societies, in this respect are striking. In the United States, government intervention through social benefits and taxes reduced the child poverty rate (in 2001) from about 27 percent to 22 percent—not an insignificant reduction, but one that still left us with the highest child poverty rate in the developed world. In the United Kingdom, by contrast, an almost equally high poverty rate, around 25 percent before government spending, was brought down to about

15 percent by more generous government expenditures on the poor. That rate is still very high for an affluent country; in countries like Sweden and Finland, the effect of government benefits is even more striking. Sweden's recent poverty rate would have been about 18 percent in the absence of government policies to reduce it, but those policies—which are very generous in Sweden, as in many Northern European democracies—brought their child poverty rate down to roughly 4 percent, dramatically low by comparison with the United States or even the United Kingdom (UNICEF 2005).

In some countries, like Switzerland and the Netherlands, poverty rates among children are low even in the absence of heavy government spending. In contrast, many of the countries of the developing world, and some in Eastern Europe and the former Soviet Union, are characterized by extremely high rates of poverty before government intervention *and* minimal efforts by government to reduce poverty through social benefits, which helps explain the depth of inequality and social exclusion within them.

It is common, both in the United States and elsewhere, to hear harsh criticism of the "welfare state." Generous social spending is said to have all kinds of negative effects, especially on economic growth (although it is not so easy to actually see those effects in the affluent societies of, say, Scandinavia). But whatever one may believe philosophically about the virtues of spending to help vulnerable people, it clearly has an effect on rates of violent crime. It isn't accidental that not a single one of the Northern European welfare states has a high level of violent crime. In that sense, violence must be seen as a cost of some societies' reluctance to provide similar supports—their unwillingness to commit themselves to providing all of their residents with at least a minimal standard of well-being, a universal floor below which no one is allowed to fall.

We can see this relationship from another angle if we juxtapose rates of infant mortality—that is, the proportion of infants who die before they reach their first birthday—with rates of death by violence across different societies. Infant mortality is an important issue in itself, but it also reflects a society's commitment to providing health care to everyone, including the most vulnerable, whatever their economic situation—and thus also serves as a more general indicator of a society's commitment to social inclusion. As Table 3 illustrates, infant mortality

TABLE 3 INFANT MORTALITY AND HOMICIDE RATES

	Infant Deaths per 1000 Live Births	Homicide Deaths per 100,000 Population
Russian Federation	16	21.6
Latvia	10	11.6
Estonia	8	14.8
UNITED STATES	7	6.9
Canada	5.4	2.6
United Kingdom	5.3	0.8
Australia	4.8	2.1
Greece	4.8	1.2
Switzerland	4.3	1.1
Germany	4.2	0.9
Portugal	4.1	1.1
France	3.9	0.7
Czech Republic	3.9	1.4
Norway	3.4	0.9
Sweden	3.1	1.2
Finland	3.1	2.2
Japan	3.0	0.6

Source: Infant mortality data from UNICEF, *Innocenti Report Card Number 7*, 2006: Homicide rates from World Health Organization, *WHO Report on Violence and Health, 2002.*

rates and homicide rates are revealingly linked. The United States' infant mortality rate (like its homicide rate) is startlingly high for an affluent country, at about 7 per 1000—considerably higher than much less affluent countries like Greece, Portugal, and the Czech Republic, and even more distant from other highly affluent countries like Japan, Sweden, Norway, and Finland, all of which have infant death rates less than half the U.S. rate (and homicide rates that are dramatically lower).

At the other end of the scale, countries like Russia, with an infant mortality rate of more than 16 per 1000, or Latvia, at 10 per 1000, suffer even higher levels of homicide than the United States. In some countries in Latin America and the Caribbean, the rates of both infant mortality and homicide are even higher.

In some countries, much basic social support is provided by local communities, extended families, or employers rather than more formally by government. Historically, that has been true in Japan and some of the countries of southern Europe, like Greece or Spain. But the effect is similar. The evidence suggests that it's not so much *who* provides social support to vulnerable people as the sheer fact that *someone* does that is most important in sustaining a sense of social cohesion and blunting the sharpest edges of the kind of deprivation that leads to violence. It's particularly troubling, therefore, that these traditional, informal means of social provision are weakening in many societies as a result of economic changes and shifts in social policy while very little is being put in their place as an alternative. Whether formal or informal, these social supports have been rooted in cultural traditions that stress the importance of mutual support and collective responsibility. Today, those traditions are increasingly being challenged, around the world, by more competitive and individualistic values. One of the troubling consequences of that shift may be the erosion of an important source of protection against the forces that breed violent crime.

D. STRAINED FAMILIES

All of these problems—economic inequality, poverty, marginal work, and poor social supports—also profoundly affect another crucial institution: the family. This is particularly important in understanding violent crime for two reasons: One is that a very substantial part of violent crime takes place *within* the family—between parents and children, or between intimate partners. It is violence behind closed doors, or what in Latin America is sometimes called *la violencia privada*—private violence. Because this kind of violence is often hidden, we usually understate its magnitude. In many countries, violence against family members is widely accepted as normal; even in countries where it is not, and where there are strong laws and public policies against it, much of it still flies beneath society's radar. But it is a problem of enormous destructiveness, and one that is at crisis levels in some countries.

Families are also important in understanding the roots of violence because they are the institutions that most influence the kinds of people we become—how we grow and develop as human beings. We are not, after all, just a collection of isolated individuals who spring up fully formed—violent or gentle, predatory or compassionate—at birth. We grow up in social settings, of which the most important—at least when we're very young—is the family. It's in the family that we learn the rules that are designed to guide our behavior and the cultural and social values that shape our personalities and our relationships with others. It is where we learn the moral beliefs that distinguish right from wrong in our culture, learn how to manage frustration and anger, and much more. It is also the place where we come to feel loved and cared for—or not; to feel reasonably secure and confident in our sense of who we are and what we are worth—or not. So it is not surprising that what happens in the family has been shown repeatedly to have a powerful effect on someone's chances of becoming involved in violence.

This point is sometimes taken to extremes, by both scholars and the public. Some argue that bad parenting is the main or even the only cause of crime, and that children are either fated to be criminals, or saved from a life of crime, by the time they are six or eight years old. Sometimes, this leads to a passive abdication of society's responsibility to help families in trouble, on the ground that there is almost nothing that a society can do that will make much difference in the private and intimate world of the home. At the same time, a single-minded focus on the family has sometimes led authorities to try to "crack down" on parents in order to enforce what they take to be proper child-rearing practices. In some countries, parents have been fined if their children skip school, or if they are deemed to be acting in antisocial ways in public.

But families do not exist in a vacuum. They operate within very specific social, economic, and cultural surroundings that differ greatly both within and between societies. Those surroundings shape virtually every aspect of family life, including the capacity of parents to bring up children in ways that minimize their risks of violence.

Let's look first at one of the most tragic aspects of violence around the world: violence against children. We know that child abuse and neglect is one of the most potent sources of violence in later life, as well as being a terribly destructive and widespread violent crime in its own right. The maltreatment of children translates into later violence for many reasons: It models violence as an accepted way of dealing with conflict; it engenders anger and resentment that may later be taken out on others; at the extreme, it may damage a child physically in ways that interfere with healthy development (Daly 2007; Turner, Finkelhor, and Ormrod 2006; Widom, Schuck, and White 2006).

It is often said that child abuse happens at all levels of society, and there is an element of truth in that; but it's also true that *serious* child abuse—both in the United States and in other countries—happens much more often in some social conditions than in others. The great majority of cases of fatal child abuse in the United States, for example, take place in low-income families, particularly in families that also suffer from social isolation and a lack of outside support; and the role of poverty and a lack of support in the community appears consistently for nonfatal abuse as well. Violence against children is also closely related to long-term unemployment, especially when it is concentrated within particularly disadvantaged communities. As with other kinds of serious violent crime, child abuse tends to be found most often in communities with multiple and mutually reinforcing disadvantages. And the impact that the abuse has on a child—the likelihood that abuse will result in emotional damage or violence later in life—is also aggravated by parental unemployment and poverty (Freisthler, Merritt, and LaScala 2006; Turner, et al. 2006; Widom, et al. 2006).

Much the same pattern appears for domestic violence against women. As with child abuse, it too can take place anywhere on the social ladder. But especially in its most severe and damaging forms, domestic violence is more common where families are poor, where they are isolated from outside support and observation, and where women are economically vulnerable and unable to support themselves on their own; and therefore less able to escape dangerous or abusive relationships. Where women are enmeshed in supportive extended families and have the educational and economic resources to support themselves, they are less likely to suffer abuse. Social isolation, deprivation, and marginalization, in other words, not only create the conditions that may lead men toward violence in the home, but also close off the kinds of opportunities that might allow women to escape it (Krug, et al. 2002; Michalski 2004; Purvin 2003). These connections have been found in countries around the world, from the most affluent to the poorest (Koenig, et al. 2006). As one recent study of domestic violence in Chile puts it,

> It appears that certain common risk factors or indicators of vulnerability for domestic conflict transcend national, cultural, and racial boundaries. Balancing elevated levels of economic and life stresses when raising young children in poverty may increase couples' vulnerability to spousal violence around the world. (Ceballo, et al. 2004, 299)

Beyond the specific problems of child abuse and domestic violence, social exclusion and economic deprivation also interfere with parents' ability to care for children in ways that could reliably insulate them from violence (and other problems) as they grow up. The result, as a recent report from the Council of Europe notes, is "a vicious circle whereby one failure leads to another, each aggravating the others" (Daly 2007, 92–93).

> Isolation, a lack of resource persons in their immediate circle, social and emotional vulnerability, insecurity, poverty, and physical and mental illnesses build on each other and weaken a person's parental ability.

Parents who face the stresses and insecurities of poverty or unemployment on a daily basis may become hopeless, depressed, or angry—all of which can interfere with their ability to raise children. Parents who have to spend long hours getting to and from work, or have to take on two or three jobs in order to put a roof over their children's heads, cannot be there to provide the consistent monitoring and supervision that many scholars believe are crucial in keeping children away from crime. Parents who are forced to move often, who are frequently uprooted from extended family and friends and therefore have to fall back on their own resources, are at special risk—particularly if there are no public policies in place to replace the informal supports they have lost.

As this suggests, societies that have done more to protect families from the destructive effects of marginality and exclusion are likely to be ones with less family violence and, in general, a greater ability to sustain the kinds of family relationships that foster the healthy development of children. It's not surprising, therefore, that some of the advanced societies in Northern and Western Europe with the most supportive systems of income maintenance, health care, and other social services are among those with the lowest levels of violence, in or out of the family. We've already seen that these countries spend more on social supports in general: the same is true for their spending on children and families specifically. The proportion of GDP spent on public benefits for families and children ranges from around 15 percent in Denmark to about 5 percent in Mexico and the United States (UNICEF 2005).

Many of these relatively generous affluent countries—along with some less-developed ones—have also created specific policies designed to ease stresses on families and to allow parents to spend more (and better) time with their children, particularly when they are very young. Many countries, for example, provide paid family leave from work that allows parents (usually fathers as well as mothers) to take off time from work, with pay, after the birth of their children, or if the child is ill or otherwise needs special care, without losing income. In Sweden, either parent can receive up to 90 percent of their usual salary for the first few years of the child's life, and somewhat less up until age 8. Similar policies, although not quite as generous, exist in many other European countries, in Canada, and in some advanced Asian and Pacific countries—as well as some developing countries, including Costa Rica and Chile.

The situation is very different in the United States. Although we did pass a national family leave provision during the 1990s, it provides only for unpaid leave, and that for only 12 weeks. Some states (and individual employers) have gone further, but none have yet approached the generosity of the provisions in many other advanced industrial societies. A recent study of family leave policies in 173 countries found that 169 of them provided some "guaranteed leave with income to women in connection with childbirth" the remaining four countries were Papua New Guinea, Swaziland, Liberia, and the United States (Heyman, Earle, and Hays, 2007).

Many countries also have national provisions guaranteeing child care for very young children—often subsidized substantially by government funds. In the United States, child care for most working parents is generally available only on a private basis, is often cripplingly expensive, and—apart from some particularly generous employers—heavily subsidized only for people who are receiving some kind of public assistance. In many countries of the developing world, the situation is considerably more desperate than that. When it comes to childrearing, families are dependent on their own resources and the informal support of friends and extended families at a time when, in many places, these sources of potential support are being eroded by rising inequality and migration.

The impact of these national differences in family policy has recently been illuminated in a report from the United Nations Children's Fund (UNICEF 2007) on the well-being of children in twenty-one industrialized countries. The report shows that on a variety of measures—including material well-being, family relationships, and health and safety—some countries in the developed world score strikingly worse than others, in ways that match up, interestingly, with what we've seen about their relative levels of violence. Overall, the

Netherlands ranked at the top, closely followed by Sweden; other high-scoring countries included Denmark, Finland, Spain, Switzerland, and Norway. At the bottom were the United Kingdom and the United States, which scored considerably lower than such poorer countries as Portugal, Greece, the Czech Republic, and Poland.

The study also specifically attempted to measure what it called the "quality of family and peer relationships," combining the percentage of children living in single-parent families or stepfamilies, the percentage who ate their main meal with their parents more than once a week, and the percentage who reported that their parents spent time "just talking to them." (It also included a measure of the proportion of children reporting that their peers were "kind and helpful.") By this measure, some countries—including Italy, Portugal, the Netherlands, and Switzerland—were very much above the average, and several others, including Ireland, Greece, Spain, Norway, Denmark, and Belgium, also ranked highly. The United States and the United Kingdom again ranked at the bottom of the list. As this suggests, it was not necessarily the wealthiest countries that scored well on the quality of family relationships; some less-affluent countries did much better (a point to which we'll return).

These differences in family support shed light on the much-debated question of the relationship between family disruption and violence. One of the UNICEF report's indicators of family well-being, again, was the proportion of children living in single-parent families. There has long been a great deal of controversy about whether children in those families are at greater risk of being involved in crime and violence than those who grow up in two-parent families. The issue is complicated, especially because the condition of being a single parent—particularly a female single parent—is so closely bound up with other things that we know increase vulnerability to violence, including higher risks of poverty, social isolation, joblessness, and the absence of strong social supports. Teasing out the independent contribution of being in a disrupted family is therefore very difficult. The best assessment of the evidence is that growing up in a family with two married parents does offer some protection against violence, juvenile delinquency, and the likelihood of being incarcerated (see, e.g., Harper and McLanahan 2004; Lauritsen and Schaum 2004; Schwartz 2006).

All other things being equal, in short, there are advantages to growing up in a two-parent family versus one broken by separation or divorce or, even more, one in which the parents never married in the first place. But that finding must be kept in perspective. Most research, for example, confirms that more important than the structure of the family is the quality of the relationships within it, coupled with the quality of the outside social supports available to it. Even more important, the chances of winding up in a "broken" family, or one in which the parent was never married, are themselves crucially shaped by the wider social and economic context. Communities wracked by high levels of marginal work and poverty, for example, are ones where creating and sustaining a marriage is unusually difficult. Societies that provide little by way of economic and social supports for vulnerable families are likely to be ones where rates of out-of-wedlock childbearing and family breakup are high. On all of these counts, unsupportive and unequal societies tend to both breed fragmented families and make the conditions of those families more precarious, more stressful, and more volatile.

The UNICEF study of child well-being sheds some light on this connection. The percentage of children living in single-parent families is very small in some of the lower-crime countries of Europe, including Italy, Greece, Spain, Belgium, Portugal, and Ireland; but relatively high in others, notably the Scandinavian countries. It is higher still in the United States, and also high in some countries of Eastern Europe, like

Russia, Latvia, and Estonia—again, all societies with high levels of violent crime.

More than 90 percent of children in Greece and Italy live in two-parent families versus just 60 percent in the United States. The stability of families in countries like Greece or Spain may well be one of the reasons why they have managed to maintain relatively low levels of serious violence historically (though, as in other countries, a good deal of violence, especially in the family, may be hidden). In the Scandinavian countries, the pattern is different: although the rate of single parenthood is relatively high, the potentially troublesome effects are countered, to an important extent, by the generosity of public supports for families, especially single parents and their children. Strikingly, for example, the rate of poverty among single-parent families in Sweden is considerably lower than that for *two*-parent families in the United States, primarily because of the very generous income benefits Sweden offers such families. In contrast, the United States—along with some of the countries of Eastern Europe—suffers from a particularly devastating combination of widespread family disruption coupled with low levels of public support for single-parent families. It's in this combination, in fact, that we may see one of the most important sources of America's unusually high rates of violent crime, for it means that all too many children in the United States are growing up in conditions stripped of both informal and formal support.

The quality of family life, however, is influenced not only by social and economic conditions, but by deep-seated cultural traditions as well–traditions that shape the beliefs and values people hold about raising children and about the relations between men and women. Some of these traditions are very relevant for understanding patterns of violence around the world.

Much research, for example, suggests that severe physical punishment is likely to increase the risks of later violent behavior in children subjected to it. Although it may have a short-term effect in stopping a child's bad behavior, it is not effective over the long term in instilling the kind of internalized moral values that could keep young people from violence in the future. At the same time, it may contribute to later violence in the same ways that serious abuse does: by modeling precisely the sort of behavior that we wish to avoid, or by generating feelings of resentment and anger in children that may later be taken out on others. As a recent report from the Council of Europe puts it,

> When parents use a physical means of controlling and punishing their children, they communicate to their children that aggression is normal, acceptable and effective—beliefs that promote social learning of aggression . . . . [Corporal punishment] is not effective and is potentially dangerous. It humiliates the child and engenders feelings of revenge. It also convinces the child that fighting is the right way to solve conflicts. (Daly 2007, 46)

And a attitudes toward the use of physical punishment vary greatly around the world. In some countries, including the United States, corporal punishment is widely (although by no means uniformly) accepted as a normal part of childrearing, and legally allowed not only in the family but, in many states, as a means of discipline in the schools. The same is true, on an even more intense level, in some of the countries of Latin America, the Caribbean, and other parts of the developing world. As we've seen, these are among the world's most violent societies. On the other side, as of this writing, at least 14 countries have formally prohibited all corporal punishment of children, even in their homes. Sweden was the first country to do so: It banned corporal punishment altogether in 1979, after having banned it in the schools as far back as the 1950s. Germany banned corporal punishment in the family in 2000. A number of other European countries—including very affluent ones like Denmark, France, Norway, Austria, and Finland, but also somewhat unexpected ones like the Ukraine, Croatia, Latvia, and Romania—had banned it by 2004. In some cases, including Sweden, the formal prohibition of corporal punishment came after many years of its increasing informal rejection by the public.

There are similar variations in the cultural tolerance of violence against women by their husbands or by other men. In many countries it is still considered acceptable—or even mandatory—to punish women for what are considered to be transgressions against male authority or against the integrity or honor of the family. Surveys suggest that in some countries, remarkable percentages of both men and women support a husband's right to beat his wife for a variety of presumed infractions, ranging from talking back or disobeying them to refusing sex (Krug, et al. 2002, 94). In New Zealand, only 1 percent of men say it is all right for a man to use violence against his wife when she refuses him sex; in rural Egypt, a startling 81 percent of *women* agree with that statement. One percent of men in New Zealand and 4 percent in Singapore believe it is acceptable for a man to use physical violence against his wife if she talks back or disobeys him, versus up to 50 percent of men in some parts of India and fully 78 percent of women in rural Egypt (Krug, et al. 2002). The more recent WHO multicountry study of violence against women found that although more than three fourths of women in some countries—including Japan and Serbia/Montenegro—felt that violence by a partner was *never* justified, only one fourth or less in rural Bangladesh, Peru, Samoa, and Ethiopia agreed. Almost 80 percent of women in provincial Ethiopia—but very few in Japan, Serbia, or even urban Brazil—believed that wife-beating was justified if a woman disobeyed her husband (WHO 2005, Ch. 2, 5). Not surprisingly, research in many countries consistently links such attitudes to higher rates of violence against women (for example, Koenig, et al. 2006).

But these cultural attitudes justifying violence in the home are not separable from the structural social conditions that surround families and that shape relations between the sexes. Attitudes that support domestic violence tend to be more common in poorer countries of the Third World and among poorer groups within more affluent countries—although, of course, hardly confined to them. They are bred and sustained by insecurity, marginality, and the stresses of lives lived with limited resources, limited opportunities, and limited chances for dignity and respect. But once established, these attitudes can take on a life of their own, persisting even when external conditions change, and adding to the mix of forces that breed violence behind closed doors.

E. HARSH AND INEFFECTIVE JUSTICE SYSTEMS

In some places, the criminal justice system has itself become an important part of the violent crime problem. On the surface, this sounds counterintuitive: after all, the criminal justice system is supposed to control crime, not aggravate it. But we have long understood that harsh criminal justice policies can exacerbate crime. And there is troubling evidence that this process is increasingly at work in some countries today.

The idea that the criminal justice system can "backfire" in this sense has a long history. It was part of the critique leveled by what some people consider the earliest criminologists—the so-called *classical school* of criminology—in the eighteenth century. Looking around them, these critics saw a system that was heedlessly and, in their view, needlessly harsh. They believed that a violent and punitive system of criminal justice would only harden the attitudes of the people who were subjected to it, and ultimately erode the legitimacy of government as a whole. These ideas, radical at the time, led to the equally radical view that punishments should be made proportionate to the crime, a view that, of course, has been fundamental ever since to democratic systems of criminal justice.

Beginning around the 1930s, many American criminologists again took up the idea that the experience of being sent to prison or a juvenile institution could make criminals worse: angrier, more alienated, and less capable of fitting back into normal society. And there is now an impressive body of empirical research that backs up this argument. For a variety of reasons, many of the people put behind bars emerge from their punishment more likely to commit crimes than they were when they went in. This is especially likely if they have been treated badly on the inside, if they have not been helped to overcome the problems that got them involved in crime and sent to prison in the first place, and if they go back to the same outside conditions from which they started.

This becomes especially relevant for understanding global differences in violent crime when some societies turn to mass imprisonment as a main instrument of crime control. Beyond a certain point, the disproportionate investment in punishment and the huge numbers of people who move in and out of the prison system become themselves a crucial part of the mix of conditions that breed violent crime. The justice system becomes deeply entwined with—and an important contributor to—the constellation of larger inequalities and disadvantages suffered by some individuals and communities: an engine that works to perpetuate social exclusion.

As mass incarceration has risen in many countries around the world, this is becoming a problem of global significance (Stern 2005); but it has gone much farther in some countries than others—most notably the United States, the world's leader in incarceration. Research points to several related ways in which the vast growth of imprisonment may contribute to the problem of violence.

First, mass incarceration aggravates the problem of what I've called *marginal work*. People with prison records are at the bottom of the job queue—the end of the line—when it comes to getting employment. The problem is especially severe for young people. Teenagers who are incarcerated—who are often those with the fewest opportunities for solid work to begin with—see even those limited opportunities shrink after prison; research suggests, in fact, that being locked up as an adolescent has a negative impact on their future that is as great as dropping out of high school (Western, Pettit, and Guetzkow 2002). With close to one in three young black men who have dropped out of school in prison or jail at any given point (Western, Pattillo, and Weiman 2004, 1), this has created a classic vicious cycle: Youth who grow up in badly disadvantaged communities with poor schools and minimal opportunities for inclusive work are already at the tail end of the job market, and are at a very high risk of committing crimes. If they then do commit crimes and go to prison, their already low chances of finding inclusive work are diminished still further, which makes them more vulnerable to becoming involved in crime again, and so on. All of this helps explain why roughly 30 percent of black men who do not go to college spend some time in prison during their lifetimes (Western, et al. 2004, 1). In some neighborhoods the proportion of men who go to jail or prison at some point is far higher (Cadora 2007). The criminal justice system does not necessarily start this spiral of ever-increasing marginality, but it does exacerbate it, and makes it far more difficult to escape.

Partly because of its effect on employment, mass incarceration also has powerful adverse effects on families and communities. The wholesale incarceration of men who come disproportionately from a handful of the most deprived communities means that those communities lose people who are fathers, uncles, brothers, and husbands—potential sources of economic and social support and parental guidance. It can, of course, be argued that many of the men who go to prison weren't doing these things very well even before their incarceration, and their presence may even have been dangerous for their partners and children. But as researchers have increasingly shown, it cannot help matters that some of the communities with the fewest social resources routinely lose even more by the removal of such a large proportion of their residents, especially working-age men. And the growing rate of imprisonment of women, again heavily concentrated in some of the country's most disadvantaged communities, means that many more children are growing up without parents at all, or growing up with parents who have been effectively "disabled" by their prison experience (Clear 2007; Johnson and Waldfogel 2004; Rose and Clear 1998).

In a country where, at any given point, well over two million people are behind bars and far more go through the prison system at least once at some point in their lives, the failure of that system—or any other institution—to address the problems that got them there in the first place by investing in effective treatment or reentry becomes extremely significant in explaining the magnitude of the crime problem. This issue will obviously be less significant in a society where relatively few people go to prison to begin with, but in the United States, where hundreds of thousands of inmates are released each year, it is a large and growing issue. Most of those released inmates return to a relatively small number of communities that are characterized by concentrated and often extreme disadvantages. There are few opportunities for jobs or training, even for young people who are not saddled with the experience of going to prison. They are usually areas that have been steadily depleted of both public and private investment: communities with limited health care, meager social services, and few stores. They are also places where formerly incarcerated people are likely to be surrounded by conditions that greatly increase the risks of being pulled back into crime—a thriving drug trade, a flood of guns, and the presence of many other people in the same marginal situation. Those would be difficult conditions to overcome even with serious investment in programs to help returning offenders, but with only scattered exceptions, that investment has not been made, and that failure must now be ranked among the most important causes of violent crime in America.

In all these ways, the United States' penal system contributes to the larger inequalities and processes of social exclusion and marginalization that breed violent crime. And the resort to mass incarceration exacerbates those conditions in more indirect ways as well. The societies that invest a disproportionate amount in prisons tend to be among those that invest the least in the kinds of social policies that increase social inclusion and solidarity and decrease inequality and exclusion. Excessive investment in prisons draws public resources away from more constructive social purposes. Money spent on expanding the prison system is money that cannot be spent on such things as preventive health care, mental health services, income support, or job creation. We see this in stark relief in the phenomenon of so-called "million dollar blocks" in some American inner cities: single city blocks that soak up more than a million dollars a year in public funds to incarcerate the startling number of offenders who live in them (Cadora 2007), money that could have gone to provide preventive social services, create jobs, or improve the quality of education.

At the extreme, the existence of a vast penal system serves as a bulwark against more constructive social change and social action. The prison system becomes a place where, in effect, a society's social problems may be swept under the rug—a politically acceptable alternative to dealing with the deeper social strains and divisions that perpetuate violence. To the extent that it does so, it hinders the kinds of changes that could reliably reduce violence in the long run.

This is not, of course, a uniquely American problem. It also surfaces in other countries—such as Russia, for example, our closest "competitor" in incarceration rates. One Russian criminologist estimates that fully one fourth of Russian men have at one time or another been confined in the country's vast penal system—which apparently does even less to reintegrate offenders than the American system does (Galinsky 2006). It is also a serious problem in some of the countries of Latin America, where prison populations have risen sharply along with high rates of violence in recent years. In Brazil, for example, overcrowded and volatile prisons feed into deep-rooted problems of street violence, gangs, and drug dealing, and many prisons are themselves places of extreme violence (Stern 2005). Even in some of the countries of Western Europe, prison populations have sharply increased in recent years, often in tandem with rising levels of relative poverty and growing inequality.

Overreliance on prisons is not the only way in which a society's criminal justice system can encourage violence. In some countries in the developing world, the police and courts are so poorly developed, inadequately funded, or corrupt that they cannot reliably uphold the law or provide citizens with effective protection against crime. In extreme cases, violent criminals may operate with impunity, and entire communities can be overwhelmed and demoralized by gangs and drugs. In the absence of reliable institutions of public safety, people may take the law into their own hands in self-defense, a strategy that often amplifies the violence. In some places, this weakness of public systems of justice is just one aspect of a larger problem: most public institutions in those countries, including education and health care, suffer from inadequate investment and policies designed to shrink government in the name of economic growth—policies that quickly become self-defeating when public health and safety disintegrate as a result.

F. EASY AVAILABILITY OF FIREARMS

The three students murdered in Newark in the summer of 2007 died of gunshot wounds. They joined roughly 12,000 other Americans, on average, who have met that fate every year for the past several years.

In the United States, we take for granted that there are huge numbers of firearms in the hands of civilians, and many Americans argue that the right to own and carry them is fundamental to our Constitution and our way of life. In most other advanced industrial societies, the situation is very different. Guns are far more strictly regulated than they are in the United States, and in some countries many kinds of guns are now for all practical purposes banned from civilian ownership—most notably the United Kingdom, which banned most handguns in 1997 and has since extended the prohibition to other kinds of firearms as well (Australia, Canada, and Brazil, among other countries, have also tightened gun regulations considerably in recent years). Such is the disapproval of guns in the United Kingdom that, with some exceptions, even the British police typically do not carry them, and many say that they would quit their jobs if they were forced to. Most other advanced industrial societies have not gone as far along this road as Britain has, but they have gone much farther than has the United States, which has been mostly moving in the other direction in the last few years, passing laws making it easier for citizens to carry guns, to conceal them when they are carried, and to use them in situations of conflict or threat. Of an estimated 875 million privately held firearms in the world, the United States alone accounts for roughly 270 million (Small Arms Survey 2004).

Not surprisingly, many people argue that this is an important reason for America's unfortunate preeminence in violent crime, especially homicide. Guns encourage people who are tempted to break the law by tilting the equation of force in their favor, and gunshots are much more likely to cause serious damage or death than fists or even knives, other things equal. So what might otherwise have been a simple schoolyard fight becomes a hospital emergency; what might otherwise have been a broken nose becomes a fatal gunshot wound.

On the surface, the bare numbers support this interpretation. We've seen that the United States—the advanced industrial country that makes the least governmental effort to control guns—is also the one with the highest levels of serious violent crime, and especially of homicide; and guns are involved in vast numbers of those crimes. Most young people who die of violence in the United States die by gunshot, and for every American who dies from gun violence, another four, as we've seen, wind up in the hospital.

There are, to be sure, gun killings and injuries in other advanced countries—but, as Chart 4 shows, there are far fewer of them than in

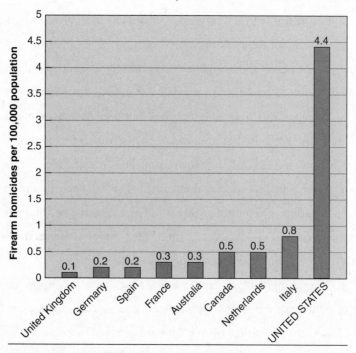

CHART 4   FIREARM HOMICIDE RATES, SELECTED COUNTRIES
Source: Data from Krug et al, 2002: figures for various years around the turn of the 21st century.

the United States. The other countries with high levels of gun violence are mostly in the Third World, especially in Latin America and the Caribbean and parts of Africa. According to one recent survey, Latin American and Caribbean countries alone account for roughly 40 per cent of an estimated 200,000 gun homicides annually around the world: Western Europe accounts for about one percent (Small Arms Survey 2004, 177). The gun homicide death rate in the United States is forty-four times that in the United Kingdom, twenty-two times that in Spain and Germany, and fourteen times that in France.

Many people believe that America has a high level of gun deaths because it is a New World or "frontier" society, but Australia and Canada, also frontier societies in the New World, have gun homicide rates that are, respectively, one-fourteenth and one-ninth of ours. In 2006, the state of Alabama reported 247 firearm homicides—57 more than in the entire country of Canada.

Critics would argue, however, that the relationship between guns and violent crime is not so simple. They would say that this view presumes a kind of simplistic technological determinism: If guns are accessible, they will be used to hurt or kill other people. But most people who have guns don't use them to commit crimes, even in the United States; and in some countries a high prevalence of guns goes along with a low rate of violent crime and, especially, a low rate of homicide. The two countries most often mentioned in this respect are Switzerland and Israel. In both, many ordinary citizens have to serve in the military and traditionally have been required to have guns of their own. Yet neither country has a high rate of civilian gun violence, and both have rates of homicide that match those of most Western European countries.

This doesn't mean that there is no connection between gun ownership and violence in those countries. More than two thirds of domestic homicides in Switzerland are committed with firearms, most often with a military weapon that is stored in the home; research shows that in general there is a strong correlation between household gun ownership and the risks of violence (Eisner and Killias 2004), suggesting that there is indeed a link between violence and the presence of guns, even in a country with relatively little violent crime overall. Yet it remains true that even with guns easily available, Switzerland maintains a very low rate of violent gun crime.

Meanwhile, there are also countries where very high rates of violence generally, and of homicide specifically, go along with relatively low rates of gun ownership in the civilian population. The most striking example is Russia, where, according to one estimate, only about 10 percent of homicides are committed with guns, versus roughly two thirds of homicides in the United States. Handguns in particular account for less than 4 percent of homicides in the Russian Federation, versus more than 50 percent in the United States. In Russia, nearly half of homicides are committed with knives, compared with just 13 percent in the United States. Another large portion of Russian homicides involve "bodily force"—mainly fists or feet (Pridemore 2006). This picture may change in the future, because traditionally strong gun controls in Russia are now weakening under the impact of a flourishing trade in firearms. But the pattern, shared by some other Eastern European countries, shows that it is possible for a modern society to have a high rate of violent crime that is only marginally connected to guns.

So the critics have a point. The sheer presence of guns does not necessarily mean that they will be used in violent ways, nor are guns a necessary prerequisite for high rates of violence in a given society. But the argument misses a more important and more complex point about the relationship between firearms and violence: The role of guns in violent crime cannot be considered in isolation from other conditions that influence the likelihood of violence, such as the degree of inequality, the depth of social exclusion, and the erosion of family and community supports. In a relatively peaceful, egalitarian, and cohesive country like Switzerland, few people shoot someone else, even if they have the technological means to do so because guns are widely available. But in a country already wracked by the kinds of adverse social conditions that predictably breed violence, the easy availability of guns adds fuel to the fire, and can take on a life of its own, creating a destructive spiral of violence, retaliation, defensive gun carrying, and more violence.

Where young men are sufficiently marginalized that they feel a need to assert themselves violently against others in order to gain respect, the easy availability of guns means that serious injury or death is far more likely when they do. Where many young people are sufficiently damaged that they are driven to lash out at others for real or imagined slights, the fact that there is likely to be a gun at home, or one for rent for $20 an hour down the street, can turn a teenage staring contest into a tragedy. Where a combination of "macho" cultural attitudes, economic insecurity, and weak family support breeds a high level of domestic violence, the routine presence of guns in the home can turn a kitchen quarrel into a fatal encounter. Where poverty and bleak opportunities for legitimate work breed a flourishing drug trade, a flood of guns greatly increases the lethality of the violence that predictably goes with it.

This helps explain why some European cities that suffer from their own deep problems of joblessness and social exclusion still have relatively low levels of homicide by American standards. One example is Glasgow, Scotland, one of the poorest cities in Western Europe, which has long suffered high rates of youth violence, but mostly involving knives and fists, not firearms. The city's homicide rate, although high by European standards, is still low by American standards, and the relative lack of easy access to guns is probably an important part of the explanation. Indeed, something similar is true for cities in the United Kingdom generally, where inequality and poverty rose sharply in the 1980s and early 1990s and, although there have been partly successful efforts to reduce them more recently, remain more severe than in other affluent European countries (Pantazis, et al. 2006). According to most measures, crime—including serious violent crime—also rose, as we would predict, as those problems deepened. But the homicide rate remained very low in the United Kingdom throughout this period, and indeed, was among the lowest in the developed world. It's a reasonable assumption that the low availability of guns was part of the reason for the unusually low rate of fatal violence in circumstances that would have been expected to increase it.

There are, of course, guns in England for those sufficiently motivated to find them, and in recent years several highly publicized youth gun killings have taken place there. That is surely a tragedy, but by United States standards it is a tragedy that remains remarkably infrequent. It is sometimes argued that the systematic effort to ban guns, and especially handguns, in England has led to an increase in violent crime, but this argument appears to have it backward, at least when it comes to homicide and gun injuries.

Thus, whatever you may believe philosophically or morally about the virtues of gun control, it's hard to avoid the conclusion that in conditions that are otherwise conducive to breeding violent crime, the wide prevalence of guns compounds and "lethalizes" those problems. The relative absence of guns is no guarantee that a society with high levels of social disadvantage and exclusion will not be wracked by violence, as the Russian example shows; but their presence in those conditions practically guarantees that it will be. Once again, this drives home the point that the forces that breed violence are deeply intertwined. The United States has a massive problem of gun homicide not just because it has a massive number of guns, but because it has a massive number of guns *and* harsh economic and racial inequalities and weak social supports and large numbers of marginalized youth and a flourishing drug trade—among other things. It is this combination that conspires to make the United States resemble countries like Brazil or El Salvador, where a similar volatile combination of widespread social adversity and abundant firearms prevails.

It's important to understand that even if there were far fewer guns in the United States, our level of violence would still stand out as unusual among the advanced societies of the world. Keep in mind that aside from homicide, most violent crime in the United States is not committed with guns. Of the roughly 1.6 million nonfatal assaults that landed someone in a hospital emergency room in 2004, only about 50,000 involved gunshot wounds. Only about one fourth of robberies and 3 per cent of rapes, according to the victim surveys, involve firearms (U.S. Bureau of Justice Statistics, 2006).

The American homicide rate itself, moreover, would remain unusually high even in the absence of guns. We've seen that the United States leads the world—or at least all of the countries for which we have reliable statistics—in homicide among children under five. Yet only a very small proportion of those homicides are committed with firearms. Small children die from being beaten, shaken, and otherwise terribly maltreated, but they are very rarely shot to death. More generally, even if every gun in the United States were to suddenly disappear, the overall American murder rate would still exceed that of almost every other developed country. The death rate for non-gun killings alone in the United States—just under 2 per 100,000 in 2004—surpassed the rate for all homicides combined in all but two of the other advanced industrial countries of the world.

Among young men—who are, again, the group at the highest risk of death by homicide in the United States (and in many other countries as well)—the United States non-gun homicide death rate of 3.2 per 100,000 is triple the overall youth homicide rate in France, four times the overall rate in Germany and Switzerland, and more than six times the overall youth homicide death rate from all weapons in Austria and Japan. In short, even if we assume, just for the sake of illustration, that in the hypothetical absence of guns none of the firearm killings in the United States would take place by other means—a highly improbable assumption—the United States would still be at the top of the list for violent death in the advanced industrial world.

Of course, that's only a thought experiment. In the real world, the United States is awash in guns, and the prevalence of guns cannot be separated from other aspects of American culture and social policy that have contributed to the country's unusually high level of violence. The resistance to regulating firearms is one more example—along with minimal public spending on income support, health care, child care, job creation, and other preventive social services—of a more general reluctance to challenge the sway of market forces in determining the conditions of people's lives. Just as some Americans think that no one should have to pay taxes to support programs designed to help the most vulnerable people in our society, some also believe that no one should be allowed to infringe on the right of gun manufacturers and dealers to sell their products without government regulation, even if this means that communities already made volatile by deep economic and social adversities are simultaneously flooded with the tools of deadly violence.

CONCLUSION: THE TWO FUTURES OF VIOLENCE

The issues we've touched on are complicated, but we can sum up the basic lessons very simply: Where people are well cared for; where they have something meaningful to do in their lives that brings them respect and a sense of contribution as well as a measure of economic security and well-being; where they are treated well and fairly by authorities, including those in the criminal justice system; where they have the support of stable communities and nurturing families and can envision a future of the same kind for themselves and their progeny, they are unlikely to commit violence against one another.

The societies that are routinely torn by violent crime, in contrast, are harsh societies, and they are harsh in many ways at once. They foster economic policies that create insecurity and deprivation at the bottom and that concentrate wealth, resources, and opportunity at the top. They offer few social protections for vulnerable people, and allow the struggling or the unlucky to fall through the cracks of the economy. They are typically punitive in their approach to the treatment of offenders, and often in their approach to childrearing as well. They are likely to enforce, or at least tolerate, the social and economic subordination of women. They are neglectful societies that tend to ignore social problems until or unless they explode into conflict and violence. They are societies characterized by what we might call a *culture of disregard,* in which people feel little sense of responsibility or solidarity toward others and a "me-first" ethic of personal gain often dominates public life.

These are not, of course, the only factors that are linked to high levels of violence. Others may be extremely important as well, in varying degrees in different societies. Alcohol is one. Heavy drinking has been linked repeatedly to high rates of both domestic and street violence, and societies differ considerably in the degree to which they tolerate or encourage it. In some countries—El Salvador and Colombia are prominent examples—a history of civil conflict or war has deepened social antagonisms, flooded the country with guns, and contributed to endemic levels of gang violence and drug dealing. And the illegal drug trade is, of course, deeply interwoven with violence, especially in countries characterized by wide economic inequalities and large numbers of marginalized people for whom drug dealing appears to be a rational and appealing alternative.

But the fact that we can see so many similar processes operating again and again to produce violence in very different kinds of societies in every corner of the world means that we know something about what it would take to reduce it. As I said in the beginning, the wide differences in violence tell us that the problem is not inevitable—at least on the level that it is experienced in the countries that suffer it the most. The success of some societies in reducing violence offers lessons that we can build on, if we choose to do so.

But whether we will make use of what we've learned is an open question. Too often, in fact, we seem to be moving in precisely the wrong directions if our goal is to reduce the potential for violence around the world. In many countries there is a movement toward policies that—in the name of the "free market" or "economic rationality" or "globalization"—promise to exacerbate the conditions that breed violence and to weaken the institutions that protect against it. The social arrangements that are characteristic of the most dangerous societies are now, in many places, being enshrined as fundamental virtues: the tolerance of great inequality in the name of economic growth; a willingness to let individuals and families fall into extreme deprivation in the name of encouraging "personal responsibility"; a willingness to leave people's well-being up to the fluctuations of the job market; the shrinking of public supports for the vulnerable in the name of boosting self-reliance and ending dependency.

These policies are often justified on the ground that they will lead to faster economic growth, and ultimately improve the quality of life for everyone. But as we've seen, growth by itself doesn't necessarily translate into greater social well-being. It's true that it is much better, other things equal, for a society to be affluent than not; but abundance without the spread of equality and social support, affluence that is confined to some and denied to others, won't do the trick. Simply growing richer will not diminish violence if it is accompanied by widening social divisions, the exclusion of many people from a chance to enjoy the fruits of growth, and the weakening of the potentially protective institutions of community and family. But although the record tells us that this model of social and economic development has great costs, it is where many societies around the world appear to be going today. The sudden imposition of free-market principles in Russia and other societies of Eastern Europe and the former Soviet Union in the 1990s resulted in skyrocketing unemployment, deepening poverty and economic insecurity, and the shredding of existing social safety nets, along with rising violence, infant mortality, physical illness, and alcoholism, creating what one scholar describes as "an explosive mixture of distrust, social degradation, exclusion and further social division" (Karstedt 2003, 309). In China, a similar sharp turn toward individualistic and profit-oriented priorities in a country that had formerly been based on a more communal social model spawned massive joblessness, destroyed rural communities and livelihoods, and created a floating population of the economically disconnected and disaffected, along with rapidly rising rates of crime (Liu and Messner 2004). In Latin America, the 1980s and 1990s witnessed a widespread social and economic crisis brought on by what one observer (Ayres 1998, 14) calls an "exclusive" process of growth, including the reduction of social spending and the adoption of policies of "structural adjustment" mandating that already poor countries in the region cut back on essential public spending and social services. The result was deepening poverty at one end, increasing wealth at the other, and desperate conditions for large numbers of the urban poor.

In the United States, an only slightly less extreme pattern has prevailed. Economic inequality has reached unparalleled heights in recent years, as the very well off have become even more so while the poor have not gained. The destructive effects of this trend are compounded by America's historic legacy of racial subordination and the equally stubborn ideological resistance to using public investment to remedy social problems. That combination has brought us inner cities that are all too often left adrift in conditions that have become extremely dire—communities that in a very real sense have become increasingly abandoned by the larger society, and are caught in a downward spiral of social exclusion, violence, and mass incarceration.

Other advanced industrial societies have not gone as far down that path, but in many of them, the historic commitment to a vision of social inclusion has begun to weaken. Inequality has risen in many advanced countries as wages for working people at the bottom of the income scale have fallen and social transfers from government have been scaled back in the name of trimming what are seen as the excesses of the welfare state (UNICEF 2005).

In a predictable response, the criminal justice systems of many countries have expanded in order to contain the consequences of widening social divisions, growing poverty, and the spread of youth marginality. No developed country has gone as far in this respect as the United States, where the already outsized prison population doubled since 1990 alone; but some are moving in that direction, adopting precisely the policies that have helped give the United States its distressing combination of stubbornly high violence and a swollen penal system. In England and Wales, there were roughly 45,000 inmates in prisons in 1992; fifteen years later, there were more than 80,000. In the Netherlands, the prison population nearly tripled in those years, from slightly more than 7,000 to more than 21,000, raising the incarceration rate from 49 to 128 per 100,000 (Downes and van Swaaningen 2007). In some developing countries, the increases were even greater. In Brazil, there were roughly 114,000 prison inmates in 1992 and more than 400,000 in 2007, a rise from 74 to 211 inmates per 100,000 population. In Mexico, simultaneously with fundamental social upheavals and deepening inequalities, the prison population shot up from about 86,000 in 1992 to 216,000 in 2007 (ICPS 2007).

At the same time, rates of incarceration in some other countries were stable and in a few cases declining during this period: Sweden, Finland, Canada, Switzerland, Slovenia, France, and Italy, among others, fit this pattern. We seem to be seeing an increasing division between those countries that are struggling to maintain their longstanding commitment to low levels of incarceration coupled with high levels of social provision and support for their citizens versus those that either never had those traditions or are beginning, under the spur of economic ideology, to weaken or abandon them.

Why, if these policies seem so obviously destructive, are we moving in these counterproductive directions? I believe there are several reasons. One is that the social costs of these policies are only rarely talked about in ways the public can understand, so we continue to define those costs as resulting from the problems or pathologies of the people who are hurt by these policies, rather than as consequences of the policies themselves. Closely related is the fact that the costs of these policies are borne increasingly by people who have little voice or political influence, while the benefits go disproportionately to people whose influence is great. Those who set these destructive social forces in motion are the least likely to be hurt by them, whereas those who bear the brunt of the costs are increasingly isolated and decreasingly visible.

This polarization is deepening as serious violent crime appears to be becoming even more concentrated than before among the "losers" in the global competitive race. We can see this phenomenon both in high-violence societies and those with traditionally low levels of violent crime. In the United States, for example, the disparity in the risks of violent death between the poor and the affluent has grown markedly in the past generation. Children in the bottom fifth of the population, who already had a 76 percent higher risk of dying by homicide than those in the top fifth in 1969, had a 159 percent higher risk by the year 2000 (Singh and Kogan 2007). In Sweden, a very different society with much narrower social divisions and a much lower level of serious violence, a somewhat similar polarization has taken place in recent years, such that violence resulting in the need for medical attention has become seven times as likely among the poor than among the rich (Nilsson and Estrada 2006).

This increasing concentration means that violence may come increasingly to be seen as a problem for "those" people rather than for "us," and thus not a matter of great urgency. But it would be tragic if these developments were simply allowed to continue. Reducing violence was one of the great achievements of civilized countries in modern times, an achievement that went along with diminishing poverty, the reduction of needless illness, and many other social advances. If we want to reduce the destructive impact of violence in the future, we will need to build on the positive lessons we have learned from that experience, not ignore them. The danger is that we will instead go backward, rolling back those gains even where they have been most enduring.

So there are choices to be made, and they are not just abstract ones. The hard fact is that if we continue to tolerate or encourage the conditions that we know breed violence around the world, many people will die and many more will be injured, physically and emotionally. And they will not be picked randomly, as in a lottery, but will be drawn disproportionately from those who have traditionally been the most frequent victims of violence: the young and the poor, people of color, those most left out of the global competition for the good life. The choice is stark and simple: We can either let that process continue and fortify ourselves against it, with more gated communities and more prisons, or we can decide that it is not tolerable and work to change it. What we cannot do is pretend that we don't know it's happening.

REFERENCES

Ayres, Robert L. 1998. *Crime and Violence as Development Issues in Latin America and the Caribbean*. Washington, D.C.: The World Bank.

Benson, Michael L., John Wooldredge, Amy B. Thistlethwaite, and Greer Litton Fox. 2004. The correlation between race and domestic violence is confounded with community context. *Social Problems* 513:326–42.

Blau, Judith and Peter Blau. 1982. The cost of inequality: metropolitan structure and violent crime. *American Sociological Review* 47:121–28.

Bourgois, Philippe. 2002. *In Search of Respect: Selling Crack in el Barrio*, 2nd ed. Cambridge: Cambridge University Press.

Brown, Michael K., Martin Carnoy, Elliott Currie, Troy Duster, David B. Oppenheimer, Marjorie M. Shultz, and David Wellman. 2003. *Whitewashing Race: The Myth of a Color-Blind Society*. Berkeley and Los Angeles: University of California Press.

Butchart, Alexander and Karin Engstrom. 2002. Sex- and age-specific relations between economic development, economic inequality and homicide rates in people aged 0–24 years: a cross-sectional analysis. *Bulletin of the World Health Organization* 80(10):797–805.

Cadora, Eric. 2007. Justice reinvestment in the U.S. In Rob Allen and Vivien Stern, eds., *Justice Reinvestment: A New Approach to Crime and Justice*. London: International Centre for Prison Studies.

Casey, Erin A. and Paula S. Nurius. 2006. Trends in the prevalence and characteristics of sexual violence: a cohort analysis. *Violence and Victims* 21(5):629–44.

Ceballo, Rosario, Cynthia Ramirez, Marcela Castillo, Gabriela Alejandra Caballero, and Betsy Lozoff. 2004. Domestic violence and women's mental health in Chile. *Psychology of Women Quarterly* 28:298–308.

Centers for Disease Control (CDC). 2004. Homicide trends and characteristics—Brazil, 1980–2002. *Morbidity and Mortality Weekly Report* 53(8):169–71.

———. 2007. National Center for Injury Prevention and Control. *Injury Mortality Report*. www.cdc.gov, accessed August 2007.

Chamlin, Mitchell B. and John K. Cochran. 2006. Economic inequality, legitimacy, and cross-national homicide rates. *Homicide Studies* 10(4):231–52.

Clear, Todd R. 2007. *Imprisoning Communities: How Mass Incarceration Makes Disadvantaged Communities Worse*. New York: Oxford University Press.

Cullen, Francis T. 1994. Social support as an organizing concept for criminology. *Justice Quarterly* 11:527–59.

Currie, Elliott. 1985. *Confronting Crime: An American Challenge*. New York: Pantheon Books.

———. 1997. Market, crime, and community: toward a mid-range theory of post-industrial violence. *Theoretical Criminology* 1(2):147–72.

———. 1998. *Crime and punishment in America*. New York: Henry Holt.

———. 2003. Of punishment and crime rates: some theoretical and methodological consequences of mass incarceration. In Thomas G. Blomberg and Stanley Cohen, eds., *Punishment and Social Control*, 2nd ed. New York: Aldine deGruyter, pp. 483–94.

Daly, Mary, ed. 2007. *Parenting in Contemporary Europe: A Positive Approach*. Strasbourg: Council of Europe.

DeFronzo, James. 1997. Welfare and homicide. *Journal of Research in Crime and Delinquency* 34:395–406.

Downes, David and Rene van Swaaningen. 2007. The road to Dystopia? Changes to the penal climate of the Netherlands. In Michael Tonry, ed., *Crime and Justice: A Review of Research, Vol. 35*. Chicago: University of Chicago Press.

Eisner, Manuel. 2001. Modernization, self-control and lethal violence: the long-term dynamics of European homicide rates in theoretical perspective. *British Journal of Criminology* 41(4):618–38.

Eisner, Manuel and Martin Killias. 2004. Switzerland. *European Journal of Criminology* 1(2):257–93.

Estrada, Felipe. 2001. Juvenile violence as a social problem: trends, media attention and societal response. *British Journal of Criminology* 41(4):639–55.

———. 2004. The politics of crime in high-crime societies. *European Journal of Criminology* 1(4):419–43.

———. 2006. Trends in violence in Scandinavia according to different indicators: an exemplification of the value of Swedish hospital data. *British Journal of Criminology* 46(6):486–504.

Field, Craig A. and Raul Caetano. 2004. Ethnic differences in intimate partner violence in the U.S. general population. *Trauma, Violence, and Abuse* 5(4):303–17.

Freisthler, Bridget, Darcey H. Merritt, and Elizabeth A. LaScala. 2006. Understanding the ecology of child maltreatment: a review of the literature and directions for future research. *Child Maltreatment* 11(3):263–80.

Frias, Sonia M. and Ronald J. Angel. 2005. The risk of partner violence among low-income Hispanic subgroups. *Journal of Marriage and Family* 67(3):552–64.

Galinsky, Yakov. 2006. Crime in contemporary Russia. *European Journal of Criminology* 3(3):259–92.

Harper, Cynthia C. and Sara McLanahan. 2004. Father absence and youth incarceration. *Journal of Research on Adolescence* 14(30):369–97.

Heymann, Jody, Alison Earle, and Jeffrey Hayes. 2005. *The Work, Family, and Equity Index: How Does the United States Measure Up?* Montreal and Boston: Project on Global Working Families.

Hwang, Stephen W. 2000. Mortality among men using homeless shelters in Toronto, Ontario. *JAMA* 283(16):2152–57.

Hwang, Stephen W., E. John Orav, James J. O'Connell, Joan M. Lebow, and Troyen A. Brennan. 1997. Causes of death in homeless adults in Boston. *Annals of Internal Medicine* 126(8):625–28.

International Centre for Prison Studies (ICPS). 2007. *World Prison Brief*. http://www.kcl. ac.uk/depsta/rel/icps/worldbrief, accessed August 24, 2007.

Janson, Carl-Gunnar. 2004. Youth justice in Sweden. In Michael Tonry, ed., *Criminal Justice Review Annual, Vol. 35*. Chicago: University of Chicago Press, pp. 391–441.

Johnson, Elizabeth and Jane Waldfogel. 2004. Children of incarcerated parents: multiple risks and children's living arrangements. In Mary Pattillo, David Weiman, and Bruce Western, eds., *Imprisoning America*. New York: Russell Sage Foundation, pp. 97–131.

Junger-Tas, Josine. 2004. Youth justice in the Netherlands. In Michael Tonry, ed., *Criminal Justice Review Annual, Vol. 35*. Chicago: University of Chicago Press, pp. 293–347.

Karstedt, Suzanne. 2003. Legacies of a culture of inequality: the Janus face of crime in post-communist countries. *Crime, Law, and Social Change* 40:295–320.

Klein, Malcolm W., Frank M. Weerman, and Terence P. Thornberry. 2006. Street gang violence in Europe. *European Journal of Criminology* 3(4):413–437.

Koenig, Michael A., Rob Stephenson, Saifuddin Ahmed, Shireen J. Jejeebhoy, and Jacqueline Campbell. 2006. Individual and contextual determinants of domestic violence in North India. *American Journal of Public Health* 96(1):132–38.

Krivo, Lauren J., and Ruth Peterson. 1996. Extremely disadvantaged neighborhoods and urban crime. *Social Forces* 75(2):619–50.

Krug, Etienne G., Linda L. Dahlberg, James A. Mercy, Anthony B. Zwi, and Rafael Lozano. 2002. *World Report on Violence and Health*. Geneva: World Health Organization.

Kushel, Margot B., Jennifer L. Evans, Sharon Perry, Marjorie J. Robertson, and Andrew R. Moss. 2003. No door to lock: victimization among homeless and marginally housed persons. *Archives of Internal Medicine* 163(20):2492–99.

LaFree, Gary, and Andromachi Tseloni. 2006. Democracy and crime: a multilevel analysis of homicide trends in forty-four countries, 1950–2000. *Annals of the American Academy of Political and Social Science* 605:26–49.

Land, Kenneth, Patricia McCall, and Lawrence Cohen. 1990. Structural covariates of homicide rates: are there any invariances across time and space? *American Journal of Sociology* 95:922–63.

Lauritsen, Janet L., and Robin J. Schaum. 2004. The social ecology of violence against women. *Criminology* 42(2):323–57.

Leovy, Jill. 2007. Murder stalks poverty in L.A. County. *Los Angeles Times*, August 19.

Liu, Jianhong, and Steven Messner. 2004. Modernization and reform trends in China's reform era. In Jianhong Liu, Lening Zhang, and Steven Messner, eds., *Crime and Social Control in a Changing China*. Westport, CT: Greenwood Press, pp. 3–21.

Merton, Robert K. 1957. Social structure and anomie. In *Social Theory and Social Structure*, rev. ed. Glencoe: Free Press, pp. 131–60.

Messner, Steven F. and Richard Rosenfeld. 2001. *Crime and the American Dream*, 3rd ed. Belmont, CA: Wadsworth.

Michalski, Joseph H. 2004. Making sociological sense out of trends in intimate partner violence. *Violence Against Women* 10(6):652–75.

Nilsson, Anders, and Felipe Estrada. 2006. The inequality of victimization: trends in exposure to crime among rich and poor. *European Journal of Criminology* 3(4):387–412.

Oberwittler, Dietrich, and Sven Hofer. 2005. Crime and justice in Germany: an analysis of recent trends and research. *European Journal of Criminology* 2(4):465–508.

Organization for Economic Cooperation and Development (OECD). 2005. *Health at a Glance: OECD Indicators, 2005*. Geneva: OECD.

Pampel, Fred C., and Rosemary Gartner. 1995. Age structure, sociopolitical institutions, and national homicide rates. *European Sociological Review* 11(3):243–60.

Pantazis, Christina, David Gordon, and Ruth Levitas. 2006. *Poverty and Social Exclusion in Britain: The Millennium Survey*. Bristol, UK: Policy Press.

Pickett, Kate E., Jessica Mookherjee, and Richard G. Wilkinson. 2005. Adolescent birth rates, total homicides, and income inequality in rich countries. *American Journal of Public Health* 95(7):1181–83.

Pitts, John, and Tarja Kuula. 2006. Incarcerating young people: an Anglo-Finnish comparison. *Youth Justice* 5(3):147–64.

Pratt, Travis C., and Francis T. Cullen. 2005. Assessing macro-level predictors and theories of crime: a meta-analysis. In Michael Tonry, ed., *Crime and Justice: A Review of Research* 32. Chicago: University of Chicago Press, pp. 373–450.

Pratt, Travis C., and Timothy W. Godsey. 2003. Social support, inequality, and homicide: a cross-national test of an integrated theoretical model. *Criminology* 41(3):611–43.

Pridemore, William Alex. 2006. An exploratory analysis of homicide victims, offenders, and events in Russia. *International Criminal Justice Review* 16(1):5–23.

Purvin, Diane M. 2003. Weaving a tangled safety net: the intergenerational legacy of domestic violence and poverty. *Violence Against Women* 8(10):1263–77.

Rose, Dina, and Todd Clear. 1998. Incarceration, social capital, and crime: examining the unintended consequences of incarceration. *Criminology* 36(3):441–79.

Rosoff, Stephen, Henry Pontell, and Robert Tillman. 2007. *Profit Without Honor: White Collar Crime and the Looting of America*, 4th ed. Upper Saddle River, NJ: Prentice-Hall.

Sampson, Robert J., and John Laub. 1993. *Crime in the Making: Pathways and Turning Points Through Life*. Cambridge: Harvard University Press.

Sampson, Robert J., Jeffrey D. Morenoff, and Stephen Raudenbush. 2005. Social anatomy of racial and ethnic disparities in violence. *American Journal of Public Health* 95(2):224–32.

Schwartz, Jennifer. 2006. Effects of diverse forms of family structure on female and male homicide. *Journal of Marriage and Family* 68:1291–1312.

Sethi, Dinesh, Francesca Racioppi, Inge Baumgarten, and Patrizia Vida. 2005. *Injuries and Violence in Europe: Why They Matter and What Can Be Done*. Rome: World Health Organization Regional Office for Europe.

Simon, Thomas R., James A. Mercy, and Lawrence Barker. 2006. Can we talk? Importance of random-digit-dial surveys for injury prevention research. *American Journal of Preventive Medicine* 31(5):406–43.

Singh, Gopal, and Michael D. Kogan. 2007. Widening socioeconomic disparities in U.S. childhood mortality, 1969–2000. *American Journal of Public Health* 97(9):1658–65.

Small Arms Survey. 2004. A common toll: firearms, violence, and crime. In *Small Arms Survey. 2004*, London: Oxford University Press, pp. 173–211.

Stern, Vivien. 2005. *Creating Criminals: Prisons and People in a Market Society*. London: Polity Press.

Sullivan, Mercer L. 1989. *Getting Paid: Youth, Crime and Work in the Inner City*. Ithaca, NY: Cornell University Press.

Teplin, Linda A., Gary M. McClelland, Karen M. Abram, and Darinka Mileusnic. 2005. Early violent death among delinquent youth: a prospective longitudinal study. *Pediatrics* 115(6):1586–93.

Thacher, David. 2004. The rich get richer and the poor get robbed: inequality in U.S. criminal victimization, 1974–2000. *Journal of Quantitative Criminology* 20(2):89–116.

Turner, Heather A., David Finkelhor, and Richard Ormrod. 2006. The effect of lifetime victimization on the mental health of children and adolescents. *Social Science and Medicine* 62:13–27.

United Nations International Children's Fund (UNICEF). 2005. *Child poverty in rich countries*. Florence, Italy: UNICEF Innocenti Research Centre.

———. 2007. *Child well-being in rich countries*. Florence, Italy: UNICEF Innocenti Research Centre.

U.S. Bureau of Justice Statistics, 2006. *Criminal Victimization, 2005*. http://www.ojp.usdoj.gov/bjs/pub/pdf/cv05

Van Wilsem, Johan. 2004. Criminal victimization in cross-national perspective: an analysis of rates of theft, violence, and vandalism across 27 countries. *European Journal of Criminology* 1(1):89–109.

Websdale, Neil, and Byron Johnson. 1997. Structural approaches to reducing woman battering. *Social Justice* 24(1):54–81.

Western, Bruce, Becky Pettit, and Josh Guetzkow. 2002. Black economic progress in the era of mass imprisonment. In Marc Mauer and Meda Chesney-Lind, eds., *Invisible Punishment: The Collateral Consequences of Mass Imprisonment*. New York: New Press, pp. 165–80.

Western, Bruce, Mary Pattillo, and David Weiman. 2004. Introduction. In Mary Pattillo, David Weiman, and Bruce Western, eds., *Imprisoning America: The Social Effects of Mass Incarceration*. New York: Russell Sage Foundation.

Westfelt, Lars, and Felipe Estrada. 2004. International crime trends: sources of comparative crime data and post-war trends in Western Europe. In James Sheptycki and Ali Wardak, eds., *Transnational and Comparative Criminology*. London: Glasshouse Press, pp. 19–48.

Widom, Cathy Spatz, Amie M. Schuck, and Helene Raskin White. 2006. An examination of pathways from childhood victimization to violence: the role of early aggression and problematic alcohol use. *Violence and Victims* 21(6):675–90.

Williams, David R., Rahwa Haile, Hector M. Gonzalez, Harold Neighbors, Raymond Baser, and James S. Jackson. 2007. The mental health of black Caribbean immigrants: results from the National Survey of American Life. *American Journal of Public Health* 97(1):52–9.

Wilson, James Q. 1992. The contradictions of an advanced capitalist society. *Forbes*, September 14.

World Health Organization (WHO). 2005. *WHO Multi-country study on women's health and domestic violence, Summary Report*. Geneva: WHO.

Yoshihama, Mieko, Julie Horrocks, and Saori Kamano. 2007. Experiences of intimate partner violence and related injuries among women in Yokohama, Japan. *American Journal of Public Health* 97(2):232–34.

INDEX